MORE APPLAUSE FOR
A Father for All Seasons

"Oh no," I thought as I greeted the delivery man at my garage door, "someone sent me a manuscript." An hour later, no farther than my garage steps, I lift my head up from the page and wipe a few tears away. I've been lost. Lost, not in Bob Welch's story, but in my own. For in this fine book, Bob has done what only great writers can do—through the telling of stories, they unlock all of our own pictures and feelings so that it is really your story you're reading about. I have a "how to" father book unread next to my bed. I tried starting it numerous times and bogged down. Welch's book meanders along with an easy, natural blend of story and reflection—most of the story being his and most of the reflection being mine. Get ready for a pleasant journey into self-reflection and useful insights.

—John Fischer
Author/Speaker/Songwriter/Singer

As an African-American male, I grew up without a father. I wish that I would have had a book like this one to read as I struggled with my two sons. *A Father for All Seasons* is a great book for any father.

—Dolphus Weary
Founder and President, Mendenhall Ministries

Bob Welch has an eye for the things that matter...the subtleties that shape life...and make a man. I've laughed (to the point of tears) and cried (yes, to tears) and relished the images. And I've grown. *A Father for All Seasons* is intensely personal and wonder-fully principled. It's for every man who wishes to father well.

—Stu Weber
Author, *Tender Warrior*
and *Four Pillars in a Man's Heart*

BOB WELCH

HARVEST HOUSE PUBLISHERS
Eugene, Oregon 97402

Cover design by Left Coast Design, Portland, Oregon

To Contact the Author

Write to:

1574 Coburg Rd., Suite 318
Eugene, OR 97401

or send e-mail to:

bwelch1@concentric.net

A FATHER FOR ALL SEASONS
Copyright © 1998 by Bob Welch
Published by Harvest House Publishers
Eugene, Oregon 97402

Library of Congress Cataloging-in-Publication Data

Welch, Bob, 1954-
    A father for all seasons / by Bob Welch.
        p.   cm.
    ISBN 1-56507-777-6
    1. Fathers—United States. 2. Fatherhood—Psychological aspects.
    3. Fathers and sons—United States. I. Title.
    HQ756.W429   1998   97-30518
    306.874'2—dc21   CIP

Printed in the United States of America.

98 99 00 01 02 / DH / 10 9 8 7 6 5 4 3 2 1

To the memory of my father, Warren,
whose son I'm proud to be.
And to my sons, Ryan and Jason,
whose father I'm proud to be.

ACKNOWLEDGMENTS

With deep appreciation to:

- My wife, Sally, for thinking of the idea for this book and for being a wonderful mother to two of its main subjects.

- My mother, Marolyn, for her willingness to share about my father, even though it hurt.

- My brother-in-law Greg Scandrett, for editing the manuscript and for sharing the struggles of a father who's lost a son.

- My late nephew Paul, for a shepherd boy's smile that still warms me.

- Dr. Rick Taylor, for saying so little yet saying so much.

- Mike Yorkey, for allowing my stories to run in *Focus on the Family* and, better yet, for being a friend.

- Ann Petersen, Paul Neville, and Kevin Miller, for editing the rough draft, which was sometimes like being the first one on the scene of a bad wreck.

- Asia Goins, George Hudson, Mac McFarland, Jeff Schulte, Larry Browning, J.C. Ownbey, Mabel Ownbey, Dan Edland, and the late Norm Edland, for sharing father-son stories from their hearts.

- The Thursday Morning Point Man Group—Ken Carson, Steve Messick, Mike Noah, Steve Panter, Tom Shattuck-Smallwood and Mark Spriggs—for bad puns and good prayers.

- Dan "Rodeo" Roberts, for helping when he didn't have to.

- The Dave boys—Quenzer and Chase—for reminding me on our Monday runs that once you're a father, you're always a father.

- And, finally, the Harvest House gang—Bob Hawkins, Jr., Carolyn McCready, Betty Fletcher, and Terry Glaspey—for their willingness to follow me into the father-son forest.

CONTENTS

V. Second Spring

To every thing there is a season, and a time to every pur-
pose under the heaven. A time to be born, and a time to die; a
time to plant, and a time to pluck up that which is planted; a
time to kill and a time to heal; a time to break down, and a time
to build up; a time to weep, and a time to laugh.

—Ecclesiastes 3:1-4 KJV

FOREWORD

A decade ago, when I became editor of *Focus on the Family* magazine, among the first people to write for me was a young man from Oregon named Bob Welch.

He was not your typical pro-family writer. Instead of being a pastor from a sun-laden state in the Bible Belt, he was a newspaper reporter from the Northwest—a place known for a gloomy abundance of rain and a glaring lack of churches. He didn't operate a ministry, stand behind a pulpit each Sunday, or have his own radio show.

What he had—and has only sharpened since—was an amazing perception of the world around him, a world that includes not only his own family but, as a reporter/editor, such diverse people as Mennonite families, 15-year-old cocaine dealers, and fathers who lost sons in Vietnam.

Ten years and nearly two dozen stories after his "Focus" debut, Bob has proven to be one of the American family's most eloquent voices.

From the poignancy of articles such as "If They Could See Us Now, Pop" about how America had changed since his wife's grandfather died in 1986, to the unbridled humor of articles such as one he wrote about himself and his sons surviving his wife's medical mission in Haiti, Bob has tugged at the heartstrings and tickled the funny bones of millions of our readers.

He has taken us on a seven-mile-long golf hole that he and his teenage son Ryan designed and played on the beaches of Oregon, shared of a family's pain and perseverance following the drowning of his 16-year-old nephew, and reported on an ethnically mixed family with 22 children.

What draws readers to him isn't so much what he says, but how he says it.

He writes with the detail of a good reporter, the wit of a Garrison Keillor, and the compassion of someone for whom relationships are a priority.

He doesn't preach. He tells stories. Real stories about real people who encounter real trials and real triumphs, sometimes through extraordinary experiences, other times through ordinary experiences. He's among the few people I know who can turn the act of hanging holiday lights into a soul-baring journey into mid-life insecurities.

A Father for All Seasons takes readers on a journey that's woven with laughter, tears, frustration, and fears. It is for every father who wants to better understand the journey he's on. For every son who seeks a deeper connection with the man who, for better or worse, has had such an influence on him. And for every mother or wife who longs to understand them both more clearly.

Over the years, Bob has occasionally come to Colorado Springs on speaking or reporting assignments; at times, his family has stayed with ours. Seeing him with his wife, Sally, and sons, Ryan and Jason, only confirms that he's the kind of person you want writing about family relationships. Though his stories are quick to point out his shortcomings as father and son, his life is a testament to how seriously he takes the roles.

As the father of a son myself, I don't care if Bob does hail from the gloomiest region—climatologically and spiritually—in the country. His words have brightened my life and, I trust, will brighten yours as well.

Mike Yorkey
Editor, *Focus on the Family* magazine
1986-1997

INTRODUCTION

Smoke from our barbecue mingled with the ponderosa pines, flavoring the summer air with that "livin'-is-easy" aroma. It was a warm August evening in 1996 and my family—my wife, two teenage sons, parents, uncle, sister and her family—lingered on the deck of a woodsy retreat. Oregon's Cascade Mountains stood guard in the distance.

It was time to end an almost-perfect weekend. Time to conclude a celebration of my parents' fiftieth wedding anniversary. Time for most of us to leave for our homes in the Willamette Valley, about two hours away.

We had spent two days leafing through a surprise memory book we had compiled for Mom and Dad—well-wishes, photos, and remember-the-time stories from their friends, some of whom they had known for most of their 70 years. We had dined together, watched old family videos together, had our photos taken together. We had watched as my parents toasted one another with gracious words of thanks, my father being so utterly selfless that he even spared us the pain of his fishing jokes (few of which were usually keepers).

Now, on this final night, my father unabashedly bragged to his brother about my 14-year-old son Jason's abilities at shortstop: "He's like a vacuum cleaner out there, Bill." Later, I saw him sitting alone on a wooden bench and handed my wife a camera.

"Here," I said, "how many chances does a guy get to have his picture taken with his dad in a beautiful setting like this?"

I put my arm around him. We beamed twin smiles, and my wife snapped the best photo that's ever been taken of us. Later, I hugged my father good-bye and told him I loved him. He hugged me good-bye and said the same thing, only using words from a more guarded generation of men: "Drive carefully, Bob." We drove off.

Two days later he was dead.

In the fall of 1996, I said good-bye to my father— someone who had a huge impact on who I've become as a person. As we scattered his ashes near the shore of a high-mountain lake that he loved to fish, I completed a cycle that had begun 42 years earlier when I entered the world with the title "Son."

Now, a year later, I've just said another good-bye: to my oldest son, Ryan—someone who's also had a huge impact on who I've become as a person. As I hugged him good-bye in his new dorm room, I, in essence, completed another cycle— one that began 18 years ago when he entered the world and, in so doing, honored me with the title "Father."

So here I stand, alone at this relational equator halfway between two poles: having just lost a father and, in a sense, having just lost a son. It is a place where millions of men have been. Where some are right now. And where many soon will be.

The day after my father died, after I had helped Mom with arrangements for the memorial service, I found myself walking around my old neighborhood, thinking about having built a boat with my father and about the day he hung the basketball hoop and about how he would whistle when he was nervous. From across the street, Ryan came up and put his arms around me.

"Dad," he said, "I don't want to lose you like you lost Grandpa." And on the same pavement on which I had once played street football as a kid, we stood there, hugging each other and crying. Father and son.

But someday—maybe today or maybe half a century from now—my son *will* lose me like I lost my father. And, in small increments, I've been losing my sons since the day each of them was born. Harsh as it sounds, that's how God designed this father-son relationship to work. It consists of a series of cycles. Phases. Constant beginnings and endings, modified by time and circumstance.

Seasons, if you will.

It is the spring of new birth, taking home eight pounds of dreams and hopes, and having that eight pounds of dreams and hopes not only amaze you with its fragile smallness, but also spit up on your neck.

It is the summer of exploration, when father and son learn about each other, about the world around them, about the facts of life and faith in God.

It is the autumn of change, when crossing a parking lot with your 12-year-old son, you instinctively reach for his hand to hold and—for the first time—he doesn't instinctively reach for yours.

It is the winter of letting go, two sets of footprints in the snow going their separate ways as fathers and sons encounter emotional distance, departure, and perhaps, death.

Finally, it is once again the spring of new birth as the cycle begins anew, though with fathers and sons playing different roles.

I've chosen the father-son relationship not because I believe it's any more important than, say, the father-daughter relationship or mother-son relationship. Instead, I write about it for the same reason Flannery O'Connor wrote about the South and Robert Service wrote about the Yukon: This is the landscape of life that I know.

Nearly every Monday while running with two friends, I round a hilly loop and go past a rocky outcropping. At its base lie a few scattered running shoes and clumps of wilted flowers. It is the spot where Steve Prefontaine, arguably America's finest middle-distance runner ever, died in a single-car accident in 1975.

When seeing this spot, some probably think of Pre racing down homestretch in front of thousands of cheering fans. I always think of Prefontaine's father, and what it must have been like to get a phone call saying your only son is dead.

At times, this book is intensely personal. To understand fatherhood and sonship requires an understanding not only of culture, time, and the Creator of this relationship, but also of yourself and your heritage.

It includes a 92-year-old baseball journal handed down from my grandfather.

It includes letters from my father to me and letters from me to my father.

And it includes entries from a journal I began writing on the day in 1978 my wife found out she was pregnant with Ryan, now 18, and a similar journal I began three years later when she discovered she was pregnant with our other son, Jason, now 15. (You'll note a decided emphasis on my first-born, a result of him being a fellow trailbreaker in this father-son journey. I've discussed this imbalance with Jason, who says he can handle it—for the price of a new computer.)

As the book unfolds, the perspective widens beyond the personal. As a journalist for more than 20 years, I've had a front-row seat into the lives of lots of people I would never have otherwise met. This book tells their stories, too.

I've followed a wealthy suburban father and his cocaine-dealing son through a decade-long adventure that ends in tragedy. And walked a cemetery with a father who still can't watch a jet take off without thinking of a son who flew off to Vietnam—and arrived home in a casket.

I've watched a self-professed "throwaway kid" love his infant son with a passion and purity that belied the man's background of abuse and abandonment, and marveled at a 73-year-old son who regularly visited his 94-year-old father, even though the father did not even recognize him.

I've received the joyous phone call that I had a new nephew and, 16 years later, received the shattering news that that same nephew was dead, swept away in an icy river.

I can never feel what my brother-in-law feels: the day-to-day ache that his late-night e-mail messages occasionally reveal. But I hope this book illuminates his experience and those of others, helps us better understand the privilege of being a father or son, and helps inspire us to be all God made us to be.

No two experiences will be alike. For though we're bound by our common roles, every father and every son finds himself in his own place. In his own time. In his own season.

First Spring

A time of beginnings

The year's at the spring
And day's at the morn;
Morning's at seven;
The hillside's dew-pearled;
The lark's on the wing;
The snail's on the thorn;
God's in his heaven—
All's right with the world.

—Robert Browning

In the life of fathers and sons, First Spring bursts forth in new life. It's a wrinkled baby. A guy in a surgeon's mask—also known as Dad—standing over that baby, so awestruck that he doesn't realize his video camera has been filming the floor for eight minutes. It's Little Slugger baseball pajamas.

For most, First Spring represents a blank canvas. It is an instant relationship that comes with much promise and little baggage. But for others—say, a son abandoned at birth by his father—it can be a season as cruel as the coldest winter.

It is exploring your ancestral roots. Looking back at your father's father, and your father, and your own coming of age.

It is a time of wonder. A time of firsts. A time of beginnings.

A JOURNEY
BACK

My family sits in the car, wondering what I'm doing. Wondering why, on a freeway drive from Seattle south to our home in Eugene, Oregon, we've exited in Portland and why, on a spring afternoon, I'm standing in a crack-cocaine district just north of the Rose Garden, home of the Portland Trail Blazers, staring at a brick apartment building that's guarded with iron bars. Wondering why I'm standing on the sidewalk of Williams Avenue, looking around as if I've lost something. Or someone. Which, in a sense, I have.

With no particular sense of grandeur, I've come to see my roots. Or at least some of those roots. In 1905, my grandfather—my father's father—played baseball for a school, Williams Avenue, that was once located where this apartment complex now stands. So I'm here, above all, to imagine what's no longer here. To picture a sandlot field of boys wearing shirts that don't advertise anything on them and shoes that don't look like rubber-soled, black-and-white pop art. To envision Will Adams not as a grandfather with a pipe in his mouth buying me candy watermelon slices—my lone memory of this man who died when I was eight—but as a 17-year-old boy with a mitt on his hand fielding grounders.

It is hard to imagine the horse-and-cart days of 1905 as Interstate-5 traffic drones in the distance, boom cars pulsate down the street, and razor wire guards businesses with prison-yard pride. In 1905, Orville Wright made history with a half-hour flight on the other side of the country; now, dozens of diffused jet vapor trails streak the brownish-blue sky over Portland with a redundancy that's easily ignored.

Further north, on Williams Avenue, a graffiti message bleeds from a billboard: "Kill for a living." Nearly a century has passed since Will Adams' sandlot seasons; everything's changed. But even if the journey has been jaded by time, I'm glad I've come.

It began with a small book the size of a pocket ledger. My father gave it to me years ago, long after his father had died in 1962. Written and illustrated by my grandfather, it's a yellowed journal chronicling the victories and defeats of the Williams Avenue baseball team he played on as a teenager one spring. The date written in the front of the book: April 10, 1905.

Those were the days of thick-handled, thin-barreled bats, and mitts that weren't much more than padded garden gloves. In that decade, Honus Wagner set hitting records that would stand for four decades. The hot dog was invented. "Take Me Out to the Ball Game" was written. The World Series began. And Ty Cobb—two years older than my grandfather—left the fields of Georgia to play semipro baseball for 50 dollars a month, carrying with him a pocketful of change and an edict from his father: "Don't come home a failure."

To understand who you are as a father and son, you need some understanding of who came before you. And Williams Avenue, I figure, is about as deep into the father-son forest as I can get; in fact, given what I've learned about my great-grandfather—Will Adams' father—this is as deep as I *want* to get.

Family history sometimes hurts. Who we are as fathers and sons is determined by spiritual, cultural, and experiential forces in our lives. But so, too, it is determined by the influences of those who came before us. In a sense, we are connected to our forefathers in the same way the jets over Portland are connected to the gliders that Wilbur and Orville Wright once flew over North Carolina—remotely, perhaps, yet undeniably.

Consider Cobb, a man who lived his entire life with such anger and bitterness toward other people that when he died in 1961, only three other major league players attended his funeral. He grew up under a father whose love was clearly conditional: Perfection equals acceptance. *Don't come home a failure.*

If exploring our pasts can be comforting when we discover forefathers whose legacies we're proud to share, it can be disconcerting if those legacies bring shame. But ultimately, we choose to either continue a legacy—be it good or bad—or start a new one; we may be inextricably linked to our past, but we are not slaves to it.

According to the baseball journal, my grandfather occasionally pitched but mainly played second base—the same position I played as a youth, and the same position my two sons have played extensively. He also was team statistician and, judging from his book, held that oh-so-rare position: team artist. He would play a game, compile his own box score, and draw sketches of teammates playing in baggy white uniforms with hats that made them look like police officers. His box scores were like none I've ever seen:

1 = scored
X = died on base
0 = made a good hit but was put out on base.

My grandfather finished the 1905 season with nine runs scored, three DOBs, and 14 MAGHBWPOOBs.

"I pitched first three innings," reads one entry. "Good many errors on both sides. I made the only score in the last by knocking a home run. A poor game without any double plays or science of any kind."

Another: "Teachers and half the school were up to see the game. Two cops tried to fire us off but after some pursuasian (my spelling deficiencies, this proves, are genetic) they said we might finish the game."

Reading the journal and looking at the often-comical illustrations, it was easy to imagine Will Adams' life neatly wrapped in nine-inning innocence. But when the yellowed newspaper clipping slid out from the back pages, reality slid home, cleats high. The headline is "Mrs. Welch's Serious Charges." The story reads:

> Luzetta L. Welch has made application for divorce from William J. Welch, in the state circuit court. Cruel treatment is charged, and Laura Trabaunt is named as co-respondent. The plaintiff, as specific acts, states that the defendant on one occasion threatened to throw her out of the window of their house; at another time she says he choked her, and once she claims that he beat and otherwise abused her. She also alleges that he will not let her see her child.

The plaintiff in this court case was my great-grandmother. The child was my grandfather, who was seven at the time his parents' marital land mine exploded. Laura Trabaunt, we can assume, was the "other woman."

For all that he would accomplish in his 74 years, my grandfather's greatest triumph may well have been overcoming the very man who helped give him life. For his father was an alcoholic, an adulterer, and a man whose family paid the price for his anger. After his parents divorced, my grandfather was raised by a stepfather, a Mr. Adams, whose name he took.

Generations of pain often repeat, the psychologists tell us now, but Will Adams did not repeat his past. He was imaginative, artistic, and slightly mischievous. He and his pals—guys nicknamed Happy, Gus, and Woozy, according to the journal—published their own neighborhood newspaper called the *Hooligan Gazette*. It included articles and sketches about everything from war with the Russians to a bicycle-propelled airship designed to save the Hooligan staff should they be kidnapped by Martians—cutting-edge science fiction given that, at the time, Orson Welles' radio portrayal of H.G. Wells' "War of the Worlds" hoax was still more than 30 years in the future.

Shortly after the turn of the century, a story clipped from the *Oregon Journal* newspaper, headlined "Pirate's Emblem Scares All," tells about a prank involving a skull-and-crossbones flag that had been placed over a restaurateur's house. Many took the flag to mean that someone at the house had a contagious disease and people should stay away. People panicked. The health department investigated. The police investigated. But apparently nobody ever discovered who was behind the mysterious flag: my grandfather and his Hooligan pals.

By all indications, Will Adams grew into a happy-go-lucky young man. He was known as "Whistlin' Willie," because he always had a song on his lips. Which is partly what attracted a neighbor girl, Fay Wentz.

Fay fell in love with the young man. He would come and sit on the porch swing, and when her father figured it was time for Will to go home, Fay's dad would simply switch on the porch light. Evening over.

Fay Wentz loved music; she would spend her life teaching piano and singing in church choirs. Will Adams was a hopeless romantic who channeled his imagination into romantic cards with poetry, and pen-and-ink drawings of roses and of minstrels serenading their ladies. The two fell in love and were married in 1914 in the sun room of her house on Monroe Street.

My father, the second of two children, was born in 1923. His father had become a dry-goods salesman and was often gone. But my dad inherited many of his dad's traits: He was imaginative, independent, artistic, adventurous—and yes, a serious student of pranks.

In a family scrapbook, a newspaper story next to the skull-and-crossbones item is headlined "Woman Screams;

Cops Seek Body." It describes what five witnesses thought was a possible murder—an apparent tossing of a woman into the Willamette River. It was actually an elaborate hoax spearheaded by, of course, my father.

He grew up in a house at 28th and Fremont, only a few miles from where his father had grown up and played baseball. He spent much of his youth fishing. I imagine him like Nick Adams, the young fisherman in Hemingway's "Big Two-Hearted River" short stories, only without the emotional baggage from the war.

My father liked to draw, but loved to take pictures. By age 12, he was so smitten with photography that he had turned a bedroom closet into a darkroom. He made his own pinhole cameras.

He attended Grant High School in Portland. If you've seen *Mr. Holland's Opus*, you've seen Grant High School, which was where the movie was filmed.

My dad was never a star student or star athlete; his notoriety came from less-noble endeavors, such as ramming his bicycle into the back of a parked car, flying over the top, and finding himself staring through the front windshield at a police officer.

In the summer of 1942, after graduation, he decided to go to school about 80 miles south in Corvallis, at what was then Oregon State College. One September evening before classes had started, he walked with some buddies from campus to Corvallis High School to attend a dance. He was at the drinking fountain near the school gym when he saw her: a young woman who seemed to be the human incarnation of the words the band was singing at that moment: "You smiled and then the spell was cast."

He smiled at her. She smiled at him. They danced. Danced some more. And walked home in a scene that I always imagine was something like the George and Mary postdance scene from *It's a Wonderful Life*—the college man and the high school girl.

The next day he asked her out for the evening. It was an invitation that ran head-on into one of her parents' cardinal rules: Thou Shalt Not Date College Men. She was a high school junior, and only 15 years old at that. Her parents were rigid folks; her father ran the house with the same sort of military order that he had been part of for years, and her mother was a pursed-lip sergeant-at-arms who laughed with great reluctance.

"But, Mom," she pleaded, "he's *not* a college man."

Would she really stoop to lying just to catch a movie with some city slicker from Portland? Was he really that special?

But with all the savvy of a courtroom lawyer who suddenly reveals a surprise witness, she played her trump card. "Mother, technically he doesn't register until tomorrow."

My mother's parents were stiff, letter-of-the-law types, German stock who meticulously labeled each of their garden plants, actually had a budget item labeled "Shrubs" and kept a record of every gas fill-up their cars ever made. They had great respect for technicalities.

Her mother paused. Frowned. "OK," she said, finally, "but just this once."

"Just this once" lasted more than half a century. They were married on August 11, 1946. The marriage would last 50 years and one day. It would produce my sister in 1951 and me in 1954. And, in a rather oblique way, it would explain what I was doing on that spring afternoon in 1995, standing in a crack zone in the middle of Portland, Oregon, thinking of my grandfather and father.

COMING
OF AGE

As a newspaper editor and former reporter, I often find myself learning about someone and naturally contrasting their life with my own.

I remember spending a day with Myrlie Evers, president of the NAACP and widow of murdered civil rights leader Medgar Evers, whose story was the basis for the movie *Ghosts of Mississippi*, and thinking what it must be like for a little boy to see his father gunned down in the family's driveway.

I remember covering the Pope's visit to British Columbia in 1983, and thinking how similar his bare-bones gospel message was to the kinds of messages I heard in my church each Sunday, but how his words got lost in all the pomp and pageantry and politics.

And I remember, at age 36, writing a story on fathers and sons and being reminded of something that I had taken for granted in recent years: that I was raised by a good man. Not a perfect man, but a good man. After writing the story, I wrote my father a letter.

I had forgotten having written it until my mother and I were going through his belongings after he had died. There

it was, tucked in a cedar box, along with some family photographs, a few other letters, and a handful of his favorite Far
Side cartoons. It explained much about who my father was
as I came of age.

Father's Day 1990

Dear Dad,

While researching an article for Father's Day, it occurred to me that I'm pretty fortunate having you as a father. So instead of giving you another fly-fishing book or a
bottle of Old Spice or a sailing shirt, I decided instead to
give you some of my thoughts.

I have spent the week interviewing men whose fathers
ignored them, were never home, or forced them to be something they didn't want to be, leaving their sons with a lot of
heartache that still plagues them today, decades after they
have left home.

I remember a different father. I remember a father who
took me to games, drew pictures of football players for me,
and told jokes, a few of which were funny. I remember a father who built a boat with me, took me fishing, and took
movies of me running, skiing, skimboarding, playing football, playing baseball, and swimming.

You weren't perfect (but then, neither was I). When
we'd go fishing, sometimes we had to get up too early and
stay too late. But here's the thing: You took me fishing. A lot
of sons have never been fishing with their fathers.

When building the boat, you wound up doing most of
the work. But here's the thing: You built a boat with me. A
lot of sons have never built a boat with their fathers.

When playing basketball, you had a Neanderthal-
looking set shot that hardly ever went in the hoop. But
here's the thing: You played basketball with me. A lot of
sons have never played basketball with their fathers.

Here's what I like about you, Dad: You don't pretend
you're somebody you're not. You don't follow the crowd.

I like that you didn't sell your soul to some company and move the family from state to state just so you could make more money to feed your ego. It was nice having roots, knowing we were going to stay put, having a place to call home.

I like that you're creative. Mom, I think, passed on to me a curiosity for the world around me, for people, places, things, all of which have helped me be a writer. But it was your eye for detail, mirrored through your photography and drawing, that has helped me capture what I see in this world around me.

I like that you let me be what I wanted to be rather than forcing me to be what you wanted me to be. Our family is made up predominantly of Oregon State people; but when I chose arch-rival University of Oregon, because of its journalism school, you never made me feel guilty. Nor were you miffed when I didn't choose to join a fraternity, even though the men in our family had traditionally been SAEs. Nor did you silently burn when I chose not to take over your commercial photography business, which you offered me more than once.

I like that you never stopped loving Mom, that you two have stuck together through good times and bad. I need that role model. Thanks for providing it.

In one sense, the days of knee football and piggy back rides are over. But in another sense, they live on. Because part of who I am today is due to the father you were to me way back then.

And because of the father you've been, it's easy to say the words that so many sons have never said to their fathers: I love you.

Your son, Bob

A few weeks ago, my barber asked what I was up to. When I told him I was writing a book about fathers and sons, he proceeded to tell me about his alcoholic father who ultimately committed suicide. And how he blamed his niece's recent suicide on his father. "He gave her the idea," he said.

In a world in which so many baby boomers speak bitterly about their tortured upbringings, mine was nothing of the sort. And yet my father and I weren't share-all pals who finished each other's sentences. True, I inherited some good traits from him. But I also inherited some not-so-good traits from him, such as impatience, occasional outbursts of anger—mainly while trying to fix something around the house—and a stubbornness for wanting to do projects my own way, even if my spouse suggests what is clearly a better way. (Pride, I'm slowly learning, is a hollow victory when you do things like hang a door backward.)

I inherited his sense of humor, his independent streak, and his boyhood penchant for mischievousness. The most blatant example of the latter came in high school when, during a Christmas concert, a buddy and I offered a friend 20 dollars if he would sprint up on stage and circle the entire choir while clucking like a chicken. Before we had time to consider the consequences of our offer, he was on the stage, clucking full circle en route to a one-week suspension. (He never did reveal his two accomplices—I always envisioned the principal grilling him under a low-hanging light bulb—and to this day, I can't watch a Christmas concert without feeling at least slightly guilty.)

In some ways, sons become their fathers; in other ways, they do not. As I grew up, I stretched in directions that were foreign to my father. Among them: playing competitive sports. For him, the only battle worth fighting was man versus fish, and really, the only noble weapon was the fly. But I grew up immersed in sports: playing them, watching them, refereeing them, and writing about them. In high school, I concentrated on two sports that I grew to love with a passion: distance running for its simplicity and gut-level courage, and golf for its variety and visual beauty. Meanwhile, my father went fly-fishing and, when really desperate, bait fishing.

We shared a love for sailing. But what my father loved about sailing was the boat itself—the challenge of equipping it and steering it to a destination. To me, the boat has been (and will always be) a means to an end, a door that opens to what I love about sailing: the experience itself.

As I came of age, probably the biggest difference between me and my father lay in the spiritual realm. My father's dad had little interest in religion, and my dad inherited the man's spiritual indifference. My father believed in God, but didn't live as if He were really necessary, except in times of deep distress, like when my mother was nearly killed in an auto accident in 1977. On more than one occasion he would tell the story of walking out of the Navy shipyard in Bremerton, Washington, in 1945, having survived World War II. "After that," he said, "I figured everything else was gravy." Translation: He had survived. Who needed God?

As I was growing up, my father saw religion as obligatory Sunday-morning service, do-gooders trying to strong-arm him into giving more money to the Methodist or Episcopal churches we attended, and prayers before meals that were spoken with all the passion you would use in giving the bank teller your account number. Our premeal blessings often sounded like one long word: *fortheesandallthymercieslordwethanktheeandblessthyholynameamen.*

Frankly, I wasn't much different from my father in the religious realm. On Sunday mornings, my "Hallelujah!" was reserved for that instant when, lying in bed, I would look at my clock and realize my parents had slept in and I wouldn't be carted off to church (where I once climbed out a window during a boring Sunday school class and, as an acolyte in the Episcopal Church, almost set fellow candle-lighter Grant Smith on fire). For a young sports fan like me, the highlight of going to church was simple: driving by the house of Tommy Prothro, the Oregon State football coach at the time. If there was a God, I figured He lived there.

As a high school sophomore, I lived the life of a lemming in patched Levi's—a brooding "nonconformist" who dressed, talked, and acted like everyone else in the late '60s. I was deep. I was profound. I not only read Ernest Hemingway, but also taped my favorite lines to the front of my bedroom bookcase. He was my hero.

Through music, through class discussions, through runs in the forest, I and others like me pondered our teenage existence. We discussed the essence of individuality and searched for a deeper meaning to life, which we usually seemed to find in individual 12-ounce cans labeled "Budweiser." We considered ourselves enlightened, even if, behind that enlightenment, we were more depressing than a Neil Young song.

Once we marched against United States involvement in Vietnam. Unlike our civic neighbor to the south, Eugene, where the University of Oregon was a hotbed of antiwar unrest, Corvallis—home of agriculturally-oriented Oregon State—was a conservative and sedentary place. Thus, protesting was not a regular occurrence like, say, the Kiwanis Pancake Feed. But we did our best. As we marched on this Saturday, I saw a classmate named Steve Carey, a gone-nuts Jesus Freak, who seemingly had a guitar surgically affixed to his back. He was standing alongside the parade route, and I asked why he wasn't marching. He said he didn't need to march for peace, because peace wasn't found in the streets, but in the heart. Huh? I didn't quite understand that, but then, Steve had always been a bit strange.

Our jock-and-hippie gang spread peace and brotherhood to everyone around us, unless "everyone" was someone we deemed unworthy of our club. Once we had a party at the home of a guy whose parents were gone for the weekend. We purposely didn't tell one particular person about the party because, well, he just wasn't one of us. But like the rest of us, he desperately wanted to belong, so he showed up on the doorstep midway through the party. We ran for cover. When nobody answered the door, he walked in and discovered dozens of us hiding behind the furniture, like cockroaches having seen the light and scurried for the dark.

That scene has stuck with me for a quarter of a century. It was a mirror. And for the first time, I didn't like what I saw.

I saw self-righteousness. Snobbery. Hypocrisy. Blindness. We were smug in our belief that we were true nonconformists, and yet we were really only a bunch of scared teenagers drifting with the tides of the times.

The next year, as a high school junior, I saw the light but didn't scurry behind the furniture. Instead, I asked what it meant. I had a good friend who cared enough about me to tell me that what I needed wasn't found in a 12-ounce can or on the "Most Popular" page of the high school yearbook.

He invited me to a Bible study. I said no. He invited me again. I said no again. "You won't regret it," he said. "OK," I said, hoping to get the guy off my back, "but just this once."

"Just this once"—similar to my mother's OK to date my father—turned into an eternity. In that gathering of high school kids, I found a reality I hadn't found elsewhere. A desire to live for something other than self. A willingness to believe God's promises, through faith, even when all the questions didn't come with gift-wrapped answers.

What I didn't find was what I thought I would: religion. Instead, I found a relationship. I didn't find shackles, but freedom. Not mandates, but meaning.

For the first time in my life, I understood Steve Carey. You could march all you wanted to help end a war—and sometimes that may be necessary—but you'll lose the battle if you think true peace is something you can attain through protests, politics, or laws. Because at its core, peace is rooted in the hearts of everyday people.

Like Blaise Pascal, the seventeenth-century French religious philosopher, I came to believe that each of us is born with a longing in his heart—a longing destined to be filled with something or someone. As I came of age, I had, on a subconscious level, tried to fill that vacuum with pieces shaped like pride, popularity, and partying, my search so subtle that nobody would have even expected I was on one. But what I learned in October 1970 was that the only piece that would fill that hole in my heart was shaped like a cross.

Years later, on a cold winter morning in 1988, I would stand at the grave of Ernest Hemingway in Ketchum, Idaho, and think of how efficiently he could build a sentence and how he won Nobel and Pulitzer prizes, and how, in the end, none of it could offset his misery as a human being; in 1961, not far from this cemetery, he put a bullet through his head.

Hemingway once wrote a short story called "Today Is Friday" about three Roman soldiers drinking in a bar after the crucifixion of Christ. Because Hemingway was my high school literary hero, I am loathe to criticize him. Still, I wish he would have had the spiritual imagination of his colleague Dostoyevsky, who would never have ended the resurrection story on Friday instead of Sunday. As the great Russian author penned in his nineteenth-century novel, *The Brothers Karamazov*: "If any one could prove to me that Christ is outside the truth, and if the truth really did exclude Christ, I would prefer to stay with Christ and not the truth."

As a teenager, such profundity was far from my grasp. And yet Jesus Himself honored not the profound, but the faithful— those who believed with childlike trust. The equation seemed simple enough, even if the choice was challenging: Either Christ was who He said He was—God himself, the risen Lord, the ultimate hope of the world—or He was not.

I decided He was who He said He was. In Frostian terms, "Two paths diverged into the wood and I, I, chose the one less traveled by, and that has made all the difference."

My father chose the other path. However, to his credit he never begrudged me my decision. Just as he had allowed me to go to the rival college, not join his fraternity, and not take over his business, he let me go my way. Not only that, but he encouraged my faith walk, even if it was a trip he didn't care to take himself.

When, a few weeks before leaving for college, I fell in love with a girl who shared my faith, my father warmly welcomed her. In a sense, Sally and my dad were kindred spirits. Just as he was independent, so was she strikingly herself.

Neither craved the spotlight. Neither was fueled by fads. And both were keenly creative, though in different ways.

She was the girl next door—technically, the girl five houses up the street. On a warm summer night, I was lying on my back in the front yard, experimenting with taking slow-shutter photographs of the moon. She was riding her Webco bicycle around the block with her older sister. It was August 1972.

I had seen her before. In fact, a few months back, my mother had noticed her walking by and suggested I ask her out.

"Mom, I'm leaving for college next fall," I had said—a rather tweedy answer that, when stripped to its core, really meant, "The girl has chicken legs."

The slow-shutter photographs of the moon turned out to be miserable failures, 8" x 10" masses of black with a streaky slice of white. But after Sally stopped her bike, we talked for three solid hours. We talked so late into the night that her father pulled up in his Olds 88, gave me and my shoulder-length hair a rather cool howdy-do, and whisked her away.

Three years later, I married chicken legs.

My father, in 1990, referred to that night in a letter he wrote in response to the one I had written him.

> Since the day I stood at the kitchen window and Sally stopped to talk—and you talked on into the evening—I said to myself, "How can any girl turn away a neat guy like you?" To her credit, she didn't.

It was one of the most candid, moving letters my father ever wrote me, beginning with a reference to his own father, who suffered from what was probably Alzheimer's disease before dying in 1962.

> Shortly before my dad died, I was up at the house on 122nd and Dad was sitting out on the lawn swing. Although he was confused, he still had his sense of humor. He didn't know who the woman in the house was (his wife), but he always knew (my brother) Bill and me. He said he felt he had let us all down. And

I assured him he hadn't and that we all loved him very much.

He replied: "I've waited a long time to hear that!" I was shocked and saddened. Guess we took each other's love for granted.

You have never neglected to let me know, however—just one of those things about you. Somehow, it seems backward that a father admires his son....

Thank you for that, Bob, and thanks for the Father's Day letter.

Love, Dad

NEW LIFE

I am in Mendenhall, Mississippi, one of the poorest towns in the poorest state in America, riding in a tattered station wagon with a middle-aged man named Dolphus Weary. He is the son of a sharecropper and the founder of Mendenhall Ministries, a Christian-based organization designed to help pull this pocket of black America out of the mires of poverty, racism, and hopelessness.

We hardly know each other. He's black; I'm white. He's from the South; I'm from the Northwest. I'm here as a representative of a Seattle-area church—a spiritual midget; he's the founder and director of a nationally reputed ministry in which our church is involved—a spiritual giant. But he treats me like a long-lost friend. And wants to show me something. *Someone*, actually.

We rumble down the rural road, past time-beaten shacks and rusted cars. Past fields of nothingness. Past gas stations seemingly trapped in time warps. Finally, we reach a one-story building. A hospital.

He rushes me inside, down a hallway, and into a room. His wife, Rosie, is lying in bed, a baby in her arms. We're quickly introduced.

Then Dolphus bends over, kisses his wife, and looks at the child. He picks up the baby, which is wrapped in a blanket. On Dolphus's face, a look of awe evolves into a smile, and finally into an all-out beam—the transition like watching a morning sunrise go from promise to perfection.

"This," he says to me, "is what I wanted to show you. This is my son."

A few months later, I am in Bellevue, Washington, among the most affluent, fastest-growing cities in the United States. I am in a high-rise hospital so swanky that the maternity ward gives new parents a complimentary bottle of champagne. And yet I witness a scene just like the one in Mississippi: a father proudly showing off his newborn son.

Two different worlds. Two different fathers. Two different sets of circumstances, but representing the same milestone: the beginning of father and son. A relationship forged. A seed transformed to life.

Spring.

A plane touches down at Sea-Tac Airport, among its passengers a tiny baby from India being delivered by a 747 stork to a friend of mine, who has adopted this child.

Spring.

An expectant mother in Haiti, nearly unconscious, is rushed by Jeep to a nearby hospital. Part of a Christian medical team on a two-week mission in the country, I watch helplessly as the Jeep leaves for the treacherous journey through mud, potholes, and rivers, and rejoice the next morning when hearing that she had arrived in time for an emergency C-section. It's a boy.

Spring.

A phone call from my brother-in-law on October 24, 1978: My wife's sister has just given birth to Paul Scott Scandrett, their third—and final—child. The same day—a cold, clear day—my wife arrives at the newspaper where I work in Bend, Oregon, and as we sit in our Datsun B-210, she tells me other news: "The test was positive," she says. "I'm pregnant."

Spring.

I want to shout. Dance. Rush through the newsroom, back to the press foreman and shout: "Stop the presses! Replate the front page! I'm gonna be a father!"

Instead, being a calm, cool, totally objective journalist whose job security might be threatened by such an action, I start a journal. And spend half that month's salary calling to tell friends and relatives the news.

The journal is actually more of a letter. A letter to my son or daughter whose sex, name, and favorite kind of pizza were unknown to me then. An intimate letter to someone I didn't even know. It begins like this:

Dear _____,

> When I was 12 years old (1966), my parents gave to me a Christmas present which I will never forget. It was a scrapbook, a scrapbook which contained mementos, letters, cards, and drawings from the time I was born. I've always cherished that because occasionally I can go back and remember what kind of child I was. That's what inspired me to write you this letter. I thought someday you might be interested in knowing what kind of child you were like. And what your parents were like. And what color your room was. And all sorts of things like that.

The journal recalls so much of what I've forgotten: how, after she broke the news to me, Sally and I prayed together in that Datsun B-210, thanking God for the opportunity to be parents and asking that He help prepare us.

How at that point, according to the medical books, the child inside Sally weighed less than an aspirin tablet, was no taller than a cardboard matchstick, and already had a well-formed jaw. (Well-formed or not, that jaw ultimately wound up helping our son's orthodontist put his children through college—probably Harvard—because of the amount of money we poured into headgear and braces to correct an underbite.)

How, at eight months pregnant, Sally still managed to hit five home runs in a whiffleball game.

How, if it were a girl, we would name her Amy Joy, using Sally's mom's middle name; and if it were a boy, we would name him Ryan Philip, using my father's middle name.

On June 21, we rushed to the hospital, thinking it was time. It wasn't. But the next day it was. The evening sky over the Cascade Mountains turned from blue to pink to black. Ryan Philip Welch was born at 10:53 P.M. on Friday, June 22, 1979. After mother and child fell asleep, I left for home.

As I walked out of the hospital, a moon—the same moon I photographed on the night I met this kid's mother—hung overhead and I saw the vague outline of the Cascade Mountains beneath the starry, starry night. I had the magical sense that the world had come to a standstill except for me, my wife, and that baby, like in plays when the background actors freeze in place. And I thought: *I am a father.*

Only I wasn't basking in some sort of spotlight of self-pride, but of unearned favor, thinking that God had allowed me—a guy with absolutely no stage experience whatso-ever—to play the supporting role in a Broadway production called *New Life.*

Thinking that on this spinning planet, where the number of people was nearly as infinite as the stars in this sky, one of those stars now bore my name. My blood. My genes, meaning he would grow up and have quarter-sized ear lobes, probably misspell *hors d'oeuvres*, and not be able to fold a road map.

Thinking that all I've accomplished somehow paled com-pared to this, which made me feel kind of guilty since *how* I accomplished this was not only fairly easy, but downright enjoyable.

I drove home from the hospital and opened the journal. With a pen, I wrote my son's name for the first time: *Ryan.* Then, on my Smith-Corona manual typewriter, I wrote:

There are places, I suppose, too beautiful to describe; feelings too wonderful to capture on paper. That is why I will probably fail miserably in trying to describe the wonder I witnessed tonight—the wonder of your birth.

Right now, at 2 A.M. as I write this, there is a baby boy sleeping away at St. Charles Hospital in a town called Bend, Oregon. There are only a handful of people who even know that boy exists. Billions don't know or care. That's OK. To me, you are a miracle.

At first, you were the color of a blackberry milkshake— a light purple. But, oh, so handsome. When you were laid on your mother's breast, you looked up at her and she said, "Oh, he's beautiful."

I couldn't stop talking about you in the delivery room. I kept looking at you, taking pictures, asking you questions. (By the way, you were a rotten interview; very evasive.)

I called about a dozen people tonight. Got them out of bed to tell them that Ryan Philip Welch, all 7 pounds, 9 ounces and 19 ½ inches of you, had come into the world.

As I look down the paths my life might take, the new worlds I might explore, and the new feelings I might feel, I know that I shall never know a day such as this. For today, my true love bore a son. My son.

FATHERLESS CHILD

Asia was worried. The Minnesota rains had gone on for days, and the floodwaters had now reached his elementary school, catching everyone off guard. Frantic school officials called parents to have them pick up their children. Buses splashed through river-like streets.

The five-year-old boy waited. Someone, he figured, would be there for him soon. Asia waited some more. Soon it was just him and a few other students. One by one, the remaining children were picked up and taken home. The water was getting higher.

But nobody ever came for Asia.

Finally, when the last child had been picked up, Asia stood alone in the driving rain and rising floodwaters. He decided he had no other choice. He trudged through the swirling waters to his empty house a mile away.

Not all father-son springs are cherry blossoms and fresh-mowed grass. Sometimes they're not remembered in photo albums, but in therapy sessions. Such is the spring Asia remembers.

When I see him in church these days, I occasionally think of that flood scene. Because more often than not, Asia, now

32, is holding his two-year-old son, Kyler, tightly in his arms. Or playing peekaboo with him. Or chasing him around the church as if Dad were Frankenstein.

Only a few people in our church realize the profundity of these moments. Realize that this father-son interplay is not some trivial time-waster but, given Asia's beginnings in life, a miracle. A testimony to a God who can sustain and change the human heart. A tribute to a young man who was betrayed by adults at every turn. And a reminder that though our childhoods will always influence our lives, we can break chains that have shackled us.

In Asia's case, the flood ordeal was among the less-traumatic examples of neglect and abuse he experienced. Not nearly as painful as the time his mother's boyfriend taught him to tie his shoes by standing over him with a belt, and snapping it by his ear each time he failed. Or the time he was thrown in a lake and told to swim, even though he didn't know how. Or the time his mom disappeared along with Stepfather Number 2—the only lesson he had left with Asia, then 12, being how to mix a cocktail.

"I don't have a single happy childhood memory," says Asia. "Not one. Sometimes my wife will talk about traditions, about how she always wanted to sit in the same spot when the family opened Christmas presents. Traditions? I remember getting up in the morning and finding half-full wine glasses and unfinished joints lying around. And drinking that wine and smoking those joints because I didn't have anyone around to tell me it was wrong. I thought everyone had a family like mine."

From the time Asia was born in 1965 to the time he was 18, the "family" moved dozens of times, sometimes with no notice at all. "I can't remember a single schoolteacher I ever had," he says.

Asia and his four siblings were fathered by four different men. His mother married at 16 and, excluding the live-in boyfriends, would marry two more times. She became a stripper. Asia's father left when the boy was three. His mother then moved in with a pimp.

Once, Asia called the man for cheating in a game of Monopoly. The man denied it. "You're lying," Asia said. The man punched Asia with a closed fist, giving him a black eye. Other times, the man would snap a bullwhip at him. Once, the man got into a physical fight with one of his "girls." He literally pulled out her hair. Another time, he got so mad he took his pit bull and threw it against the wall. It left a dent.

The house was cluttered with pornography. Events like Thanksgiving wound up in orgies. Hookers came and went, sometimes having sex with his mom's boyfriend.

Asia's ethnicity compounded his problems. His mother was white, his father African-American and Native American. He remembers the time his mother took him to a Mormon church. "You can come," said the greeter, then nodded at Asia. "He can't."

When his mother dropped him and his siblings off with her mother in Montana and left, his grandmother sent the kids to a Christian summer camp. In Asia's dark childhood, it was a burst of light.

"That summer was the first summer I ever remember having fun," he says. "We tossed around a greased watermelon, sang songs. I'd never done anything like that. Nobody discriminated against me; they accepted me. The missionaries talked about Jesus, about the importance of accepting Him into your life. I did."

But the good times didn't last. His mother returned and whisked the family off to Hawaii, where they had lived once before. She met a man from Guam. The family moved to Guam to live with the man's sister.

When their mother and her boyfriend abandoned the children, the kids found themselves living in a house with no electricity or food. They were placed in foster homes. Asia lived with a U.S. Navy family, but was leery.

"I didn't trust men worth beans," he says. "Men treated women horribly. Men were on my hit list."

But this was different. This man treated his wife with respect. Treated Asia with respect. Asia hit it off with the family.

When this family left for the United States two years later, Asia was placed in another foster home, this time with Campus Crusade for Christ missionaries. In a man named Warren, Asia found the father he had never had. "Warren was the first man in my life who didn't force me into something or hurt me or expect too much of me. All he asked was that I be respectful and get good grades."

With permission, Asia even started calling the man "Dad."

When a high-profile church leader made sexual advances on Asia, however, his confidence was once again shaken. "I was so confused. I didn't know who I could or couldn't trust. I kept expecting Warren to change. It was like: 'OK, when is he going to start hitting me or abusing me?'"

He never did. "Warren was the one man who modeled to me how to treat a woman. He modeled dependability, stability, and being a man of his word," says Asia.

Warren and his family moved back to the States, to Montana. After Asia graduated from high school and moved back to the United States, it was Warren he turned to when looking for direction. Originally, Asia was thinking about trying to find his birth father in the Los Angeles area and become a model or actor. It was Warren who reminded him of the drugs linked to that kind of lifestyle. It was Warren who encouraged him to get involved in Campus Crusade, which Asia did, traveling to Russia, Thailand, and Brazil on missionary trips. It was Warren who paid for Asia to attend Briercrest Bible College in Canada.

Bit by bit, the pieces in the Asia puzzle started to come together. A professor in the school's counseling department began having Asia talk about his past as a springboard to changing his future. In fact, he encouraged Asia to consider becoming a counselor himself. Asia earned a bachelor's degree in biblical studies with a minor in counseling. And through a mutual friend, he met a young woman from Oregon named Cathy.

They were the odd couple. Cathy's life had been everything Asia's had not. She had grown up in a small Oregon coast town and still lived in the same house. She had known her best friend since kindergarten. Her life was full of stability, trust, and tradition.

They were married in 1992. Asia went on to get a master's degree in marriage and family therapy and is now a social worker, dealing with abused children. Kyler Goins was born in 1994, and a second child, Savannah, in 1996.

"With Kyler, I did not want to be in that delivery room," says Asia. "Remember, I'd seen my mom in a lot of pain caused by different men. In a sense, when I saw Cathy in pain, I said to myself: 'I did this to her.'"

But when Kyler was born, Asia broke into tears and lifted his son heavenward. "Ever since I was growing up, I've always wanted a son—you know, flesh of my flesh," says Asia. "I suppose I want him to have everything I didn't have: consistency, someone who makes good on his promises, and just playtime. Fun."

Despite some poor choices on his mother's part, Asia credits her with at least giving him a sense of strength—that he could be whatever he wanted to be. "God had a plan for me, and by the time I was 19 or 20, I realized that I needed to fulfill that plan," he says.

A plan to treat women with respect. A plan to break the chain of fatherlessness he and his siblings had experienced. And finally, a plan to be there for his children when the inevitable floods of life swirl around them and they need someone to come pick them up.

FIRSTS

It had been my four-year-old son's first major league baseball game, and as we walked away from Seattle's Kingdome, I was lost in thoughts of my grandfather playing baseball in 1905, the nostalgia of the game, the way sports can bind together a father and son like the lacing of a well-made mitt.

"Ryan," I said, "what was your favorite part of all that you saw tonight?"

After an evening of hot dogs and home runs, of souvenirs and singing "Take Me Out to the Ball Game," after talking baseball strategy and doing The Wave, it soon became clear that what had impressed Ryan most was none of this stuff. It wasn't the color guard that performed the national anthem. It wasn't who won the game. It wasn't even the design of the teams' uniforms or the computerized scoreboard.

It was the 60-foot-long men's urinal.

"How can it be so long?" he asked.

When you are a young father, you remember such "firsts." They are the spice of springtime.

The first night your son is at home. The first night he actually sleeps at home. The first night your wife and you actually sleep when he's at home.

The first time we dangled his feet in the bone-chilling Pacific Ocean. (He laughed; that was a good sign.) The first crawl. The first step. The first time he emptied three drawers of clothes and sprinkled them with baby powder in an apparent attempt to re-create a winterized scale model of the Cascade Mountains.

The first movie (*Chariots of Fire*). The first trip to a fast-food restaurant (Taco Time). The first time, as a two-year-old, he was describing his new wagon to an equally young friend over the phone and, frustrated that she couldn't picture it, said, "Here, look at it," and pointed the phone outside toward the wagon.

The first time we bribed him to use the toilet by giving him a crayon, building block, or piece of gum should he succeed. The first time he used the bathroom all by himself and got such a prize. The first time his grandfather came out of the bathroom and Ryan cried, "Mom, get Grampa a prize! He went by himself."

The first haircut. ("I got ears at the barbershop," he told his mother.) The first "big-boy" pants. The first sibling (Ryan proudly pointing out his "brudder" Jason in the visitor's area. Never mind that he was actually pointing at the little girl two down from his brudder.)

The first sibling rivalry. The first "camping" trip in the backyard for the boys. (It's hard to feel too outdoorsy when you can hear "The Tonight Show" on the neighbor's TV.) The first camping trip in the great outdoors (Sparks Lake). The first backpacking trip. (Ryan was so small and his pack so big that he looked like he was carrying a refrigerator.)

The first round of golf. (Ry's favorite part was running through the sprinklers.) The first comment on God, after being informed that He could hear Ryan's prayers and the prayers of a boy in China at the same time: "Boy, God must have huge ears."

The first time he described the Statue of Liberty as "that lady with the big flashlight." The first bicycle.

The first day of kindergarten. The first time we asked what he had learned at school, and he peeled back both eyelids and said, "This." (Your tax dollars at work.) The first broken window with a baseball. (I offered a stern-faced look, peppered with anger; after all, this was a 65-dollar window. Later, when my wife had left, I patted him on the back and said, "Awesome rip, Ry.")

The first time Jason watched the family cat give birth to kittens. (He tried to get one of the newborns to drive his plastic Batmobile. No dice.) The first time we were at the beach cabin and I felt someone trying to pry my mouth open. "Wake up," whispered Jason. "I'm playing micro machines and your mouth is the garage." The first day the boys caught a fish.

The first detailed understanding of the Christmas story. "Dad, guess what," Jason said after Sunday school one morning, "did you know the three guys who came to see the baby Jesus—the 'Gemis'—it took them two years? And they brought him three gifts: gold, that mold stuff, and frankencider."

The first (and only) baptisms for each of the boys. The first trip to Disneyland. (It was nine years ago, but I still have the "Small World" song lodged in my brain.) The first New Year's Eve the boys made it to midnight.

Of course, firsts aren't always things you want to remember. For example, I also remember the first time we asked Ryan to get ready for bed and, in a three-year-old translation, he told us to take a flying leap.

The first time one of the boys had surgery and, though it was only a hernia, it was the longest two hours of my life. The first time the boys tried to burn down the back fence. The first time I stood them in front of a burned-down church to show them what can happen when little boys try to burn down fences and other stuff. The first time the boys experienced the death of someone near—their great-grandfather. ("Will his tractor go to heaven with him, too?" asked Jason.)

The first time you go to give your son a good-night kiss and he extends his hand to shake, as if you were some sort of foreign diplomat.

The first time you realize your sons are growing up too fast.

The first time you realize that, as you write about their growing up too fast, the oldest is only four.

THE
SMILE

In the heart of Oregon's Willamette Valley, the Ruckert home sits like a child's building block on an emerald picnic blanket. On this spring evening, from any window in the house you see some of the thousands of acres of green fields that make this valley the largest producer of grass seed on the planet. Little girls race from room to room. Cream pie awaits guests in the kitchen. No conversation competes with the evening news; there's no TV. Other than kids' bedrooms that look as if decorated by Hurricane Hugo, it all looks like something out of a Laura Ingalls Wilder book.

But contentment is an elusive thing, even in the hearts of those who call this rural refuge home. And so it was that back in the eighties, as Roger Ruckert plowed his fields and Susan Ruckert took care of the couple's two little daughters, something stirred inside both of them. A longing. Something in their life was incomplete.

They decided to adopt a child. And because they had two daughters, they decided to adopt a son. "God has adopted us," said Roger. "It seemed like something we should do. There are kids out there who don't have families, kids starving to death, kids who don't have mothers, fathers, or homes."

In December 1983, they met with an Oregon adoption agency that began searching for a child for them in Guatemala. And prayed that God would lead them to that one child.

• • •

At the same time, in Guatemala City, six-month-old Selvin Rauda was abandoned. It wasn't the first time. The first time had come when he was born and his father hadn't shown up at the hospital. In the months to follow, Selvin's mother took him to a babysitter so she could look for work in another town. Occasionally, she would return to see her son. Then one day she left him and never came back.

• • •

The Ruckerts began going through the steps toward adoption. Pre-adoption classes. Paperwork. A home study. Translating forms from English to Spanish. Fingerprints at the police station so they could prove to the FBI they were legit. Then the waiting. Not weeks. Not months. Years. Finally, expectations and disappointments as offers of children trickled in.

Good news. An 18-month-old boy was available. Would they take him? The Ruckerts prayed. Yes! They contacted an attorney they had hired in Guatemala City to handle the arrangements. They made plans to make the 2000-mile trip and pick up the little boy. They fixed up a room. Friends from church loaned them clothes. A surprise baby shower was thrown.

Then came the phone call from the adoption agency: The arrangements had fallen through. The boy's mother, from El Salvador, had returned for him. For Susan, it felt like a miscarriage, as if the boy they had never seen had died. Roger, less emotional, brooded silently as he rode his tractor around the fields of green.

• • •

In Guatemala City, Selvin's babysitter kept him for 18 months, hoping his mother would return. When she didn't, the young woman took the boy to the authorities. They placed him in the Bienstar Orphanage, where other little boys and girls without smiles rocked back and forth, in wall-to-wall cribs, waiting for someone to choose them. Or waiting to get old enough so they could leave for the streets, where the unchosen sell soap and beg for spare change in the city of 1.5 million people.

• • •

Slowly, the Ruckerts' wounds healed. In December 1986, two months after the other adoption fell through, another call came. Would the Ruckerts consider a 2½-year-old boy? They prayed. They felt God's peace. They said yes. Their new son was a little boy who had been abandoned by his father and mother.

His name was Selvin Rauda.

In May 1987, the Ruckerts flew to Guatemala City. They found him in the orphanage. What followed was not a series of Kodak moments. Selvin was malnourished. He was missing two front teeth. He did not smile.

The couple joyfully took their new son and left. They went out to eat. The boy ate and ate and ate. Then, because he was not used to eating so much food, he got carsick.

If you believe the TV insurance commercials, fathers meet their sons in soft-focus settings of bliss. This was the beginning of Roger Ruckert's relationship with his new son: after 3½ years and 5000 dollars and hundreds of prayers, an Oregon farmer in Guatemala cleaning up after a little boy that was his, but who he didn't even know.

For some fathers, First Spring is a thing of beauty.

So was Roger's.

• • •

That was a decade ago. Jordan Selvin Ruckert is now 13 years old. It has not been an easy decade for father or son. Jordan, it turns out, suffers from Attention Deficit Hyperactivity Disorder and perhaps fetal alcohol syndrome. He has struggled with school. Struggled with authority. Struggled with trust.

Regrets? Roger shakes his head no. Suffering, he says, is part of life, promised by God. He and his wife have four biological children; they did not adopt Jordan out of their necessity as much as his need, which points to the truest form of love: that which asks nothing in return.

Roger remembers growing up as a boy, following his father around on the farm, fixing fences, rounding up sheep. He imagined his son someday doing the same, and having the same passion for the land that Roger has. Jordan does not. But fatherhood comes with no guarantees. So just as he does with his tractor, patiently tilling the soil for crops that will come later, Roger plows on.

As my time with him and Susan winds to an end this April evening, dusk turns to darkness. Throughout the evening, Jordan and sister Emily, 9, have been spying on their parents and guests from outside the house. Finally, the two come inside for pie and introductions with me and my wife.

What leaves the biggest impression on me is not the young man's politeness or his pie-eating speed (which is considerable). It is something that didn't exist a decade ago, when Roger first saw his son. Something about three inches wide that transcends pain, radiates hope, and speaks of harvests to come.

It is a smile.

For a decade, Roger has tried to forge a bond with the boy with the smile—a bond he wishes could be stronger. Raising sons is difficult enough when that son is biologically yours; it is all the more difficult when you're handed someone nobody wanted. In a world of quick fixes, the wounds of neglect aren't so easily mended.

Still, believes Roger, nothing sown in the life of a child is for naught. For all the hopes and dreams that may lie unfulfilled between father and son, an undeniable truth remains: In Guatemala City, the Bienestar Orphanage is still full of little children with no smiles, rocking back and forth in wall-to-wall cribs, seeking someone to love them.

But Selvin Rauda doesn't live there anymore.

Summer

A time of discovery

I see the boys of summer in their ruin
Lay the gold tithings barren,
Setting no store by harvest, freeze the soils.

—Dylan Thomas

For fathers and sons, summer is a course in Life 101, but in a relaxed atmosphere with no midterm or finals. It's explaining how to twitch a fly. When to steal home. Where to find the fiction section of the library.

It's a time when sons ask lots of questions and fathers can still fudge a bit on the answers. A time of innocence that's often linked to the "boys of summer"—baseball players.

At the end of every summer, at least here in the Northwest, there comes one evening when a subtle chill portends a change of seasons: Fall is coming. School will begin. And, as a child, you get this small pit in your stomach, as if not wanting to let go of summer's ease and innocence.

Until then, it is a time to explore the outdoors while camping. To learn about the world. Ourselves. Each other. And God.

Above all, in the lives of fathers and sons, summer is a time of discovery.

COMMON GROUND

As summer arrives in Central Oregon, some of the 20 to 30 feet of snow on the South Sister mountain melts and makes its annual pilgrimage to the meadows below. Atop the 10,358-foot mountain, icy water trickles deep in the caverns. On the east flank, the water twists its way beneath the snow fields and creates the Green Lakes, 4000 feet below. From there, an outlet creek—Fall Creek—winds southward, past lava outcroppings, like a watery slalom course. Clear. Cold. Untouched by humans, save for the mountain climbers who will splash it in their faces and soak their neck bandannas in it. Near journey's end, it rushes down a 30-foot fall—its namesake—and finally turns from gallop to glide, meandering under a highway and across a meadow to create what's known as Sparks Lake.

Since the 1930s, in this very meadow, four generations of my father's side of the family have camped, fished, and watched for falling stars. It is not easy finding common ground among four generations that, collectively, have spanned more than a century. But this is ours: the outdoors. The smell of lodgepole pine burning on a campfire. The sound of oars dipping in evening water. The feel of a warm sleeping bag on that first night at Sparks Lake, knowing you're 5000 feet closer to heaven than when you left the city.

We learn about life in many ways: reading books, taking classes, talking to people, listening to sermons, asking questions, watching people around us, going to seminars, making mistakes. But we learn best when we immerse ourselves in an experience and let it soak into our every pore. For my grandfather, my father, me, and my sons, the outdoors has been that experience—a classroom as wide as the sky.

It is here we've learned to pitch tents and make fires and tell the difference between rainbow trout and Eastern brooks. It is here—away from the lights of the city—we've seen what the writer of Psalm 8 saw: "the work of your fingers, the moon and the stars, which you have set in place." It is here we've learned of courage, conscience, and culinary perfection, the latter manifesting itself in one of the few epicurean ensembles I can make that has more than two ingredients: the s'more (which, of course, has three).

My grandfather—my father's father—broke trail on this generational love of the outdoors. On the last page of his 1905 baseball journal, he pointed out that Williams Avenue School went 7-2 that season, then drew a picture of a ball player lounging in a hammock, one foot over the side. "Season's over," says the caption. "Now for camping." On another page: a sketch of a baseball player with a knapsack over his shoulder in a sort of postgame pose. The caption? "Back to the woods!"

My grandfather passed his love of camping on to his son, my father. I have a black-and-white photograph captioned "Fall Creek 1937." In it, a boy of 14 stands in hip waders in front of a lean-to tent, holding a foot-long trout. It is my father. To his right is his father, looking slightly urban in a white hat, age 49 at the time, three decades having passed since he sketched that baseball player dreaming of camping. To his left is my father's mother, looking Depression-esque in a sweater over a dress, her head wrapped in a bandanna.

I look at the grainy photograph and wonder, How could my father have been so young? (Fourteen.) My youngest son is now 14. What was my father like at that age?

From what I've learned, he was a character out of a Patrick McManus humor book. A kid who could relate to Rancid Crabtree, McManus's backwoods guru whose philosophies on life include: "The two best times to fish is when it's rainin' and when it ain't." A kid who, whenever we would be in the Sparks Lake area of Central Oregon, would tell me the story of his father driving him and his mother out the wash-boardy dirt road from the city of Bend in a Model-A to fish.

I look at the photograph and wonder about 1937. The picture must have been taken in late summer, given the few patches of snow on nearby Mount Bachelor. So I dig out *Chronicles of the 20th Century*—ten pounds of month-to-month history—to learn what was happening in the world about the time that photo was taken.

The Hindenburg exploded. Margaret Mitchell won the Pulitzer for *Gone With the Wind*. Amelia Earhart disappeared on a round-the-world flight. George Gershwin died. Actor Dustin Hoffman was born. The Reverend Martin Niemoeller, a leading Protestant critic of the Nazi regime in Germany, was arrested and jailed for "agitory" speech critical of Hitler. And my father and his parents camped beside Sparks Lake.

More than half a century later, sitting in a canoe with my sons in the middle of Sparks Lake, the view is not all that different from what my father and his dad probably saw in 1937: the South Sister mirrored in the lake; nubs of lava interrupting the pines just below the timberline; and rocky fingers of land jutting into the lake, peppered with grass and the orange and yellow of wild columbine.

I find comfort in that common experience. Maybe that's why the outdoors is such a wonderful teacher: like Scripture, it changeth not. Its truth endures, unfettered by time and circumstance and the pulsating cities beyond. It is a benchmark that binds generations, that reminds us, as Solomon wrote in

Ecclesiastes, that "what has been will be again, what has been done will be done again; there is nothing new under the sun."

From our canoe, I look at these mountains the way I look at my hometown: There's a memory on every block.

As a child, hiking across rocks near Bagby Hot Springs, then re-hiking and re-hiking the same trail for my father, who was filming my sister and me for his self-produced movie we all thought would take the country by storm: *Trout in the High Country*. (The film's final lines were something like: "Someday, maybe my son will show these lakes to his own boy and say, 'Good fishing, Son.'")

Peering into the depths of Detroit Reservoir and—remembering my father's story about how a new dam had forced the flooding of the old town of Detroit—imagining a city at the bottom of the reservoir like the lost city of Atlantis, fish swimming through houses and cars and grocery stores and across baseball diamonds with the bases still spiked in the ground.

Collecting bottle caps at Suttle Lake with my sister in the pre-flip-tab days of Nehi, Nesbitt, and Bubble-Up.

Running the dusty trails around Cultus Lake, always wondering about the mysterious Comma Lake, supposedly just off the trail, but a lake my father and I had never been able to find.

Learning to love fly-fishing while on backpack trips with my college pals, and feeling slightly guilty because I learned to love it apart from my father.

If my dad didn't teach me to love fishing, he did teach me other things. He showed me how to use a compass—not just the kind that tells north from south, but the kind that tells right from wrong. In these mountains, I learned from my father that when you reach your limit of ten fish, you do not hide five of the fish so the marine sheriff won't see them; you quit fishing. I learned you leave your campsite cleaner than you found it. I learned you don't ride a dirt bike around the campground because the peace and quiet of a group of people was more important than the freedom of one individual.

I also learned something about becoming a man. I was about 12 at the time, and we were camped at the west edge of Cultus Lake—a three-mile-long lake where the afternoon wind traditionally whipped the smooth waters into whitecaps. Family friends were arriving at the far end of the lake; my father, I assumed, would be taking the boat to pick them up, since our campground was only accessible by water.

"Why don't you go get them, Bob?" he asked.

"Me? By myself?"

"Sure."

My mother and sister looked surprised. Though it was only midday, a breeze had picked up and the mirrorlike water of morning was now tapping against the side of the boat, as if portending something. But that day, I drove our 14-foot boat for the first time by myself in what I remember as less of a taxi trip than a rite of passage. I don't think I realized it at the time—my sights were on simply accomplishing the task—but when my father asked me to go alone, what he was really saying was much more than "Why don't you go get them, Bob?" He was saying, "I trust you."

The trip went smoothly. I picked up our friends. As I neared the shore on the return trip, I was, in my 12-year-old eyes, no less a hero than Gus McRae and Woodrow Call after driving a herd of cattle from Lonesome Dove, Texas, to the prairies of Montana. When that boat gently nudged to a sandy stop, I had arrived. Not just as the driver of a boat. But, in a sense, as my father's son. As a man. I had proven something to him—and in front of his adult friends, no less. Though I don't recall him slapping me on the back or telling me so, I sensed I had somehow made him proud. And that is a feeling a son never forgets.

As I became a father myself, I came to these mountains and taught my sons how to whittle, how to build fires, and how to stay warm while camping at 6500 feet in June when you wake up at 5 A.M. and there is ice on your tent: Pack up the tent, drive back home, and crawl in bed.

Not all camping memories are warm ones. Once I was camping at Suttle Lake with my father and Ryan, then about six years old, for the first time. My expectations of the weekend were lofty: fresh air, time for my father and me to talk about something more significant than fish, and time for my son and his out-of-state grandfather to bond. My father and I lived 300 miles apart; this was a rare time together.

We woke up Saturday morning and my father, who hadn't smoked cigarettes in years, decided this was the weekend he would start. So much for timing. So much for fresh air. So much for modeling for his grandson. That's what irked me more than anything: he was seemingly oblivious to what message this sent to a six-year-old grandson who would soon be making life choices.

After his fifth cigarette, I couldn't stay quiet. I verbally blasted him like a high-Cascades thunderstorm. He didn't blast back. Instead, he apologized and quit smoking. But it cast a chill on the weekend that never went away. In 42 years, my father and I rarely clashed; when I was disappointed with him, it was usually because of incidents like this, when he seemed oblivious to what he had—in this case, fresh air, lungs that didn't need cancer, and a grandson who looked to him as a role model.

While he sometimes lapsed into periods of aloofness, I believe my father understood what was important in life. He rarely expressed it, however, saving most of his soul-baring for twice-a-year letters that came in response to my birthday and Father's Day gifts for him. In 1990, looking back at our lives together, he wrote this as part of a longer letter:

> If I conducted myself in a way that had anything to do with how you turned out, it was probably what I didn't do, more than what I did. A lot of dads tried to make their sons toe their mark. Once, while on Sparks Lake, I told you to do what you enjoyed and knew you could be good at. From then on the ball was in your hands, and you made it all by yourself.

I don't believe that. Despite the few times he disappointed me, my father taught me much. I've been too poor a fisherman to be tempted about exceeding a limit of trout, but if I caught ten I would stop. Why? Because he taught me to respect laws.

Whatever I've become—and sitting in a canoe, dwarfed by 10,000-foot mountains, you tend not to think of yourself as having become particularly big and important—has been less my own doing than God's doing, aided by the influences of people who came before me—and people who have come alongside me.

A few years ago, flying overhead in a jet, I saw the South Sister and microscopic Sparks Lake. The passengers around me all slept or read, oblivious to what was below. But I was a little like our old dog Jet whenever we would drive through his old hometown of Lebanon on our way to and from the mountains: Something stirred deep inside me. I looked down and tried to imagine exactly where my father and his parents had camped for that classic 1937 photo. I tried to see the route that my friends Loce, Wood, and I had taken while climbing the South Sister in 1975. And I tried to see the cove where the boys and I last camped in 1991.

In 1991, the Space Shuttle Atlantis deployed satellites on a nine-day mission. Pro- and antiabortion protesters clashed in Wichita, Kansas. Kuwait honored General H. Norman Schwarzkopf with their highest honor for defending the country against Iraq. Filmmaker Frank Capra, who directed *It's a Wonderful Life*, died. And my boys and I, like my father and grandfather before me, camped at Sparks Lake.

They would have been 12 and 9 at the time. How could they have been so young?

As I looked down from the plane, I was too far away to see the intricate way nature works. But I knew what was happening: The summer snow on the South Sister was melting and making its annual pilgrimage to the meadows below, where it would once again fill Sparks Lake and gently stir remembrances of generations come but not really gone.

THE TALK

I could no longer put it off. In June of 1989 I vowed that by the end of the summer, I would gather my two sons together and give them The Talk. They were only ten and seven at the time, but I've long believed too much information is better than not enough. At the same time, however, I have also believed that telling my children about the facts of life is a job akin to checking one's smoke-alarm batteries: important, necessary, and potentially a matter of life and death—but also easily overlooked on life's "To Do" list. For example, it's rare to see a note like this magnetically stuck to someone's refrigerator:

—Get gas.
—Take back overdue books.
—Buy stamps.
—Take dog to vet.
—Tell kids about the physiological differences
    between the male and female partners engaged
    in sexual reproduction as it relates to the
    one-flesh theme of Genesis 2:24.

And so it was that I kept my promise, but only barely. On Labor Day night, which I've always deemed the last unofficial day of summer, I walked my sons across the country road on which we lived to the McKenzie River, just up from Hayden Bridge.

The McKenzie is a magnificent river. It is cold and wild, tumbling down from the Cascade Mountains to the Willamette Valley below. I sat on a rock, next to the swirling waters, saw a Big Gulp cup wedged in a bush, and thought, *How appropriate*. I took a big gulp and started talking. I talked about men and women, boys and girls, boys turning into men, girls turning into women, good boys and bad boys, and good girls and bad girls.

The boys watched the river rush by.

I continued, using some words that I had known for decades and thought about occasionally, but actually had never said aloud.

The boys watched the river rush by.

I told them how God fit into all this strange stuff, about how He created sex (instead of spelling it out, I said it just like that, *sex*) for married men and women to share their love with one another and to create little people who would grow up into big people and then, scared to death, find themselves someday talking like this with their children.

By the time I was finished, my heart was pounding like the water tumbling over the rocks beside me. But I realized that my job wasn't finished. I had to make sure they had understood what I had said.

"Guys," I said, "I just dropped some pretty heavy stuff on you. Do you have any questions?"

Neither spoke. The evening lay still, save for the splash and gurgle of the water.

"Nothing?" I said. "There's nothing you want to ask?"

Ryan, my oldest, shook his head no. Finally, my seven-year-old spoke up.

"Dad," said Jason, "I gotta question."

"What's that, Jase?"

"How did God make this river so wide?"

It is now 1997, eight years later. God willing, my oldest will soon be on his own. And I find myself asking, What have I taught my sons? What have they heard? What have they digested? What have I modeled? What should I have said that I didn't? What did I say that I shouldn't have?

The mystery of raising children is that you can never be certain what's connecting and what's not—at least not entirely. It's like advertising. Most businesses do it—send messages to consumers to buy a product or service—but in most cases have little clue whether it worked. What hit; what didn't?

Likewise, we send messages to our children daily, hoping they'll buy into a value system we think is best for them, but in most cases have little clue whether it worked. What hit; what didn't?

Despite its obvious egotistical overtones, one of the grand moments of parenthood is when you see your child turning out like you. It is also among the more terrifying. An entry from my journal when Ryan was two:

> Today, when I brought a bundle of pine trees down from Mrs. Mac's place in the wheelbarrow, you put a little pine tree in your plastic wheelbarrow. You like to wear one of my old ties around the house and proudly announce: "Gotta go to work." And I can't wear work boots without you putting on yours. You like to mimic me.
>
> On the other hand, we were driving down Greenwood the other day when a green light turned yellow on me and I was forced to stop. While I did so, I uttered a not-so-nice word. And a few seconds later, you reminded me of what that word was, sort of like when I was a little boy and we'd stop at a place called Mountain House to get a Coke on our way to Suttle Lake and there was this mockingbird that would repeat whatever my sister or I would say, as if to mock us.

We teach our children even when we don't think school is in session. In the father-son relationship, summer vacation and spring break do not exist. We teach every day, every minute. We teach when they see us in action, hear our words, listen to our prayers, feel our frustrations.

Too often, we think our lessons are the sit-down kind, the planned-out kind, the sweaty-palmed kind while sitting on a rock beside a river. And they are. But our lessons are also how we react as a Little League coach when the ump blows a call, and how we treat our wives after we've both had rugged days at work, and what we say when we see a homeless man on the street, and what we do when the clerk accidentally gives us a dollar too much change.

Sometimes our lessons are good ones. Like everyone, I have racial prejudices I need to frequently confront. But I hope my sons—without me saying a word—have become more color-blind as they've seen the photos of their mother cleaning scabies off Haitian babies and by our attending a church with a black pastor and linking arms with a black ministry in rural Mississippi.

Sometimes my lessons are the wrong kind. As a boy, what hurt so deeply was to hear my mother and father fight; though it wasn't a common scene, the most perfect day could turn blustery cold when their relationship iced up. Without intending to, I've taught a few similarly chilly lessons to my own sons.

Our sons are sponges, quietly soaking up all we say and do. And we're not the only teacher in the classroom. Our culture is sending some messages that reinforce our lessons, and others that sabotage them: Buy this. Wear that. Do this. Do that.

If, as father-teachers, our goal is to turn our sons into clones of ourselves, we're shooting far too low. We're assuming a perfection in us that's reserved for Him. Better to teach our sons the selfless character of Christ than the flawed character of ourselves. And if, as earthly fathers, we mirror our heavenly Father, wonderful; the angels will rejoice. But if we don't, expect a visit from the mockingbird, who will constantly remind us what we're passing on.

We should not teach our sons with flash cards that do nothing but embed in their minds memorized facts. Instead, we should teach our sons to seek wisdom from the Word. We should teach them less calculation and more character. We should teach them not to blindly follow the world, but to faithfully follow the truth.

Not that any of these realizations quells my uncertainties about the job I've done in passing on such values. A lot of water has passed beneath Hayden Bridge since I told my sons the facts of life, and though I'm learning, I'm still asking questions.

Did I go to the flash cards too often? Did my sons hear what I said? Did I demand too much? Did I demand too little? Did they see even a glimpse of their heavenly Father in their earthly father? Did I say I was sorry enough?

And one final question: How did God make the river of fatherhood so wide?

BROKENNESS

L ooking back, he remembers not so much what his father said to him, but what the man didn't say. Not so much what his father did, but what he didn't do.

The kid was one of the best athletes in California: a tennis player who rarely lost in four years, a golfer who was shooting in the low 70s, an ace basketball player.

"But I can't remember my dad ever saying, 'I'm proud of you.' And I can never remember him hugging me."

Sometimes we make a father-son discovery that— snap—changes our lives in an instant. More often, those discoveries are spread out over years, sometimes even decades. They come from a number of people and experiences. They come with a price tag of pain.

For Mac McFarland, the ultimate summer of discovery didn't arrive until he had already done to his own sons what his father had done to him: valued them not for who they were, but for what they could do. In the game of life, Mac learned as a young man, performance is everything. Forget the process; results are what count. And the only worthy result is victory; the world has no room for losers. His father's motto? *Never let 'em see you sweat.*

"After a big match, he'd come up to me and say, 'Ya gotta work on that backhand.' He could never just say, 'Nice match.'"

When you're 16, you don't notice anything particularly wrong with that. You simply nod and work on your backhand. That's what Mac did.

Sports became the essence of who he was. Teachers cut him slack because he was a talented jock. Fellow students accepted him because of how hard he could hit a tennis ball.

After college, Mac transferred his winning-is-everything philosophy to the work world. He went into business with his father and the two of them—both compulsive workers—made it a lucrative one. Mac bought the trinkets of success: a red Alfa Romeo, a top-notch stereo system, a plush house.

He was 28, married, and had two small sons when he experienced Lesson One: trial by fire. In seven minutes, everything was gone. Burned to the ground, though the family escaped unharmed. "Do not store up for yourselves treasures on earth, where moth and rust destroy, and where thieves break in and steal. But store up for yourselves treasures in heaven" (Matthew 6:19, 20).

Out of the ashes of despair came Harold. He was an 80-year-old man who volunteered at a church youth group that Mac had been working with. He was a character, like someone out of a movie—an up-front guy whose brashness might have been abrasive if it wasn't leavened with so much compassion.

"Do you know what love is?" he asked Mac.

"Sure," said Mac.

"Do you know what *agape* love is?" he asked Mac.

Mac shrugged.

"Meet me at the coffeehouse tonight," said the Old Man, which Mac had come to call him.

The coffeehouse was an outreach ministry of the church.

Over a Coke, the Old Man explained to Mac that agape love was sacrificial love—love that expects nothing in return. "But," he told Mac, "it's tough for macho guys like you to experience agape love."

Mac scoffed. He was a winner. He could hit any shot that came over the net, even if it was a hot spinner like this.

"Fine," said the Old Man. "I want you to go up to the next person who walks in that door and tell them God loves them and so do you."

Mac almost spit out his Coke. But the Old Man was serious. And Mac's will to win didn't allow retreat.

"Fine," he said.

In walked the next customer: a long-haired hippie, male, stoned to the max. Fueled more by competition than compassion, Mac walked up to the guy and said, "Hey, pal, God loves you and so do I."

The hippie just stood there for a moment, Mac's words hitting him like unidentified flying objects—weird somethings that came out of nowhere and were too strange to believe.

"Do you mean that, man?" asked the hippie.

Instinctively, Mac reached for that father-taught lesson: *Never let 'em see you sweat.* Translation: Lie if you have to.

Then he glanced at the Old Man. And knew it was time to get real. He told the hippie that, actually, he knew little about love. He spilled his guts to this complete stranger. Lesson Two: "Humility comes before honor" (Proverbs 15:33).

The hippie had never experienced anything like this. Before the evening was over, he had made a commitment to Christ and flushed his drugs down the coffeehouse toilet. He had also told Mac what happened before he walked into the coffee shop: Feeling hopeless, he and a buddy had made a suicide pact. His buddy was already dead.

Mac gave up the business world and went full-time into youth ministry at a large California church. He helped build a fledgling ministry into a youth group that attracted hundreds of young people. And he was firmly in control.

Then came the raft trip. Everything went wrong. Food was lost. People were tired. Tempers flared. When it was over, Mac did something he could never remember doing.

He cried.

"My ministry," he told his wife, "is over."

"Your ministry," she corrected, "has just begun."

Lesson Three: The way up is down. "The sacrifices of God are a broken spirit; a broken and contrite heart, O God, you will not despise" (Psalm 51:17).

"What I realized that day, for the first time, was that it's OK to fail. OK to care. OK to be broken, vulnerable. All my life, my dad had taught me to keep my chin up. To hang in there. Why? So I could have his approval."

Some of that, Mac discovered, is good: the will to persevere, for example. Taken to extremes, it leads to a life of frustration. Because everyone must fail on occasion.

As a son, Mac began allowing himself to be broken. To fail. To allow God to compensate for his shortcomings instead of simply trying harder, jumping higher, running faster. But as a father, not able to see the same blind spot in himself that he saw in his father, he continued to ask the impossible of his sons.

"One son grew up and worked on the same youth staff I did. He would make a list of how to run the program that was better than the one I did. But I always found something to add. 'It's a great list, but . . .'"

The two skied together. "He was a much better skier than I was," said Mac. "But I never told him that. I never gave him enough affirmation."

As with his own father, it wasn't a matter of not loving his son. "My dad would have died for me, and I would die for my kids, but it was like the Pavlov dog. Once the sons accomplished one thing, the challenge was always set higher."

One of Mac's sons could take it no more. He confronted his father, and the two wound up going to a counselor. The sessions forced Mac to look in a mirror. Despite all that he had learned, what he saw in that mirror was a man who looked strangely like his father.

Thus, the final lesson: Knowing your deficiencies is one thing; allowing God to help overcome those deficiencies is another. "We are the clay, you are the potter; we are all the work of your hand" (Isaiah 64:8).

Mac confessed to his sons that he had not been the father that they needed. He began building them up with genuine praise—praise without a "but" on the end. For the first time, he learned to love them with no conditions attached.

He cherished the grace of God, which he credits for changing his heart. "I used to overstate where I was spiritually," said Mac. "Maybe I'd say I was 50 percent from where I need to be. Here's the difference: Now I might say I'm only 6 percent from where I need to be. But for the first time, I've recognized that God is my other 94. And together we're 100 percent."

A few years ago, Mac's father was diagnosed with cancer and had only a short time to live. Mac flew from Oregon to California to be with him in his last days. There, lying in a hospital bed shortly before dying, Mac's father gave his grown son something that in 50 years he had been unable to give, something that took an entire lifetime to learn how to do just once, something that said, "Take one and pass it on to your own sons."

A hug.

SONS AS
TEACHERS

S oon after I learned that my first book, *More to Life Than Having It All*, was going out of print, I was talking with a friend who was part of a weekly men's group at church. I knew he was a supervisor at a paper plant that did a fair amount of recycling.

"What kinds of things do you recycle?" I asked him.

"Newspaper and magazines," he said. "Books."

"Books, huh?"

"Yep."

"And what do you turn these books into?" I asked.

Besides being an awesome piano player who can explain the pretribulation rapture theory as if it were nothing more complicated than, say, the rules of checkers, my friend is also a sensitive guy of the nineties.

"Bob," he said, "you don't want to know."

"Kleenex?" I asked. He paused, trying to protect me from a tragic truth. "Well?"

"Worse."

What could possibly be worse than someone blowing their nose with the remains of a book that you had toiled over for two years? What could be worse than—

Oh no. Suddenly I realized what could be worse. The book that I had created, nurtured, and sent off into the world as if it were flesh of my own flesh could wind up being used as—as . . .

"Steve," I said, "when I wrote *More to Life,* I wanted it to be a book that touched people's lives. This wasn't quite what I had in mind."

We had a good laugh over the incident—and still bring it up from time to time—but frankly, it isn't easy having your book go out of print. In a sense, it's like a long, slow, painful death of someone dear. First the doctor prepares you with potentially bad news: Though your friend was once in wonderful health, he's slid downhill in recent months. The next few weeks are critical.

Those few weeks come and go, and suddenly the doctor writes to say your friend is terminal. It's time, she says, to pull the plug on the life-support machine. Later, you receive a letter asking what you want done with the remains.

I bought most of my remaining books and gave them an honored place in the attic, next to Christmas decorations and my wife's third-string collectible cows. Over the years, I've given some away, sold some, and used a few to prop up a desk. Once, for a tacky party we hosted, I brought down about a hundred books and replaced every book in the room with my own.

Sometimes we laugh to keep from crying. But as much as we hate the pain of defeat and loss and fear, these are the times we're most willing to let God make something more of us, the times when, as C.S. Lewis says in the movie *Shadowlands,* "We're like the blocks of stone, out of which the sculptor carves the forms of men. The blows of his chisel, which hurt us so much, are what make us perfect."

As fathers, sometimes God puts that chisel in our hands and asks us to add character to our sons—more accurately, His sons—not through physical punishment but through words and actions that those sons might see as painful. And sometimes, I believe, He puts the chisel in the hands of our sons and asks if they can, in perhaps different ways, do the same for us, the fathers.

As I write this book, I realize how easy it is to see the chipped stone from the lessons my father taught me and the lessons I've taught my sons. But I'm increasingly aware of how God has used my sons to help sculpt my character as well.

When I was 35, I applied for a newspaper job that I had dreamed of since working at the paper as a part-timer 15 years before. I was nervous. More than nervous. I was the "before" guy in the deodorant commercials.

"Hey, Dad," says Ryan, ten at the time. "Relax. Just be yourself."

At first, his words bounced off me, my self-centeredness shielding all at this moment. Anyway, what does a ten-year-old know about adult stuff like job interviews? The pressure to please? To skate your finest routine, complete with breathtaking spins and triple-axels, in front of a panel of judges, including the one from Outer Slovakia, who looks as if he just OD'd on chili peppers?

But then I reconsidered. *Relax* translates to Psalm 46:10: "Be still, and know I am God," which translates to "I belong to God." Which reminds me that my joy in life is not dependent on a job, but something deeper and permanent, which translates to peace.

Relax. Just be yourself. I liked that, I decided. I needed that. I went into the interview calm. I got the job. And learned a lesson from my son in the process.

I was camping with my family and, while eating our dinner, my nine-year-old niece got a sliver under her fingernail. She was in pain. Deep pain. She cried. Screamed. Whimpered. Her father-the-doctor got the sliver out—I think he gave her ten percent off since she's a blood relative—but she couldn't calm down.

My brother-in-law tried. I tried. Others tried. No luck. She continued sobbing, shivering uncontrollably. Then, toward the end of the dinner, we heard someone laughing. It was my niece. There, at the end of the table, was my nine-year-old son Jason "flying" cucumbers with his fork into his cousin's mouth as if the utensil were a plane and her mouth were a giggly hangar.

What impressed me at that moment wasn't so much Jason's sense of humor—though I enjoyed that, too. What impressed me was his thoughtfulness. His realization that someone needed cheering up, even if it took a flying cucumber to do it.

I was encouraged by that. And learned a lesson from my son-the-pilot in the process.

Often, the greatest gift my sons give me is perspective. Once, when the boys were elementary age, I found myself as a pawn in a union-management work dispute. The struggle played out month after month, and I was weary. Confused. I felt trapped. One evening, alone with Jason, I told him of my frustration, lamented my lot in life.

He sat there staring at his tormented father with eyes that seemed to say, "I understand." Then, according to my journal, he said, "Dad, have you ever shocked your tongue with a battery?"

Obviously, it was not the kind of question you would expect from a professional counselor. But it was just what I needed at that very moment: something to make me laugh. Something to remind me of how splendidly delicious children can be—delicious enough to offset whatever happened in a workplace that sometimes wasn't all that delicious. Something to refocus my perspective.

Over and over, they teach me. In how they discipline themselves in sports. In how they explore a tide pool. In how they, with childlike faith, believe God's promises without question.

More than once, when times have been tough, I imagine my tongue being shocked by a battery, and then I don't feel so bad.

LOVE AT
EYE LEVEL

Last Thanksgiving morning, at age 42, I pulled into the parking lot at a local middle school for our church's annual Turkey Bowl football game and was reminded of how long I had been doing this sort of thing. Two observations tipped me off: First, I wasn't fully recovered from the groin pull I had reinjured in last year's game after initially straining it the previous year. And second, the 19-year-old son of a friend of mine was sitting in the car next to me, preparing for the game by taking out his nose ring. I don't recall players showing up with nose rings 30 years ago, when I first immersed myself in sports. As I said, I've been at this awhile.

Since first playing knee football with my father at age five, I have played, coached, officiated, kept score, managed, cheered at, and written newspaper stories and magazine articles about thousands of games. I've interviewed Dan Marino in the Dolphins' dressing room, spoken with Arnold Palmer on a putting green, and talked family one-on-one with ex-NFL great Steve Largent, now a U.S. congressman. I've eaten breakfast with author-and-Walter-Mitty-of-the-sports-scene George ("Paper Lion") Plimpton. I've birdied the postcard hole, No. 7, at historic Pebble Beach. Run two marathons and the nationally known Hood-to-Coast relay. Para-skied. And sat in Nike chairman Phil Knight's sky suite at a University of Oregon football game.

I've profiled Alberto Salazar, at one point the best marathon runner in the world. Lunched with Olympic gold medalist Dick Fosbury, the inventor of the "Fosbury Flop" high-jump style. Attended NCAA Final Fours. And seen national track and field records set at University of Oregon's storied Hayward Field.

But of all these experiences, the most meaningful by far was the first one I mentioned: playing knee football with my father. Superstars come and go. Records are broken. But in a sense, a father is forever.

When a father gets down on his knees on the living room rug and allows his young son to smash into him and tackle him, what's taking place is more than fun and games and an occasional dented lamp shade. What's taking place is communion. Not communion in the spiritual sense, but in a relational sense. It is an act of sharing. Of a father humbling himself. Of a son thinking: *Even though my dad is big and busy, he has time to get down on his knees and pretend he's small.*

In knee football, the father is not dragging his son into his adult world; he's willingly entering his son's world. Relating at eye level.

In knee football, Matthew 18:3,4, or at least the spirit of the verses, unfolds. In these verses, the disciples ask Jesus who is the greatest in the kingdom of heaven. He does not say million-dollar athletes, people from the proper lineage, heavy-duty tithers, or mistake-free people. Instead, He calls a child over and says, "I tell you the truth, unless you change and become like little children, you will never enter the kingdom of heaven. Therefore, whoever humbles himself like this child is the greatest in the kingdom of heaven."

Becoming "like little children"—not to be confused with being immature—is important. If it weren't so important, why, 35 years later, can I remember the excited feeling when my dad would agree to play knee football with me on Sunday nights after "Lassie"? We would use a pair of rolled-up socks for the football. My father would almost always let me win. And I would almost always feel rotten and cry if I lost. But what those games made me feel more than anything else was important to my dad.

My father seldom let his adult world infringe on my child world. A professional photographer, he allowed me to take the bulbs out of his huge floodlights, tip the lamps toward the ceiling, and use them as basketball hoops. He filmed our local high school's football games for the coaches, and on Sunday nights, I got to watch the replays with the team. He used his artistic skills to paint me a Los Angeles football helmet, never balking at the difficulty of doing a Rams' helmet (twisting horns) as opposed to, say, the relative ease of a Penn State helmet (all white with a single blue stripe).

What was impressive about the way my father nurtured my love of sports was that athletics always meant much more to me than they did to him. My grandfather was more the athlete than my father, his youth firmly rooted in baseball, and his adult years given to a steady, if unspectacular, game of golf. A 1905 drawing of his—now hanging in my oldest son's bedroom—shows his blend of artistry, humor, and sports: a frustrated golfer stands in a sand trap, motioning his caddy for the final club in his bag. All the others lie broken in the sand.

But my father grew up much more interested in fishing, cars, and cameras than athletics. So when, as an adult, he got down on his knees to play football with me or made me a custom basketball backboard or took movies of me running a cross-country race, it wasn't necessarily for him. It was for me.

I've circled the sports universe since I was young. As a boy, upon first understanding the concept of death—that someday I would be removed from this world—I always pictured the same scene: me staring down from outer space at an Oregon State football game on a Saturday afternoon, unable to attend. The teams were playing. People were cheering. But I was permanently banned. That was a ten-year-old's vision of hell: not being able to watch his hometown college football team.

Despite my parents' lukewarm interest in sports, to grow up in Corvallis, Oregon, was to grow up with Oregon State athletics. The father of a grade-school friend, Mike Riley, was an Oregon State University assistant football coach. On Sunday afternoons, my friends and I would play football at Parker Stadium, where the Beavers had played the day before. We would sneak into Bell Field and high jump on the same pile of foam that Olympic gold medalist Dick Fosbury flopped on.

Not that I was all that good at any of these pursuits. When I was about eight years old, I heard of a competition at our local high school called the Punt, Pass, and Kick contest. I heard that if you won, you got to compete at halftime of an OSU football game, and if you won that, you got to compete at halftime of a San Francisco 49ers games in Kezar Stadium, which I had seen on our black-and-white TV. I had a vivid imagination as a child, and when I showed up at Spartan Field that Saturday morning, I was already envisioning myself shooting the breeze with John Brodie, the 49ers quarterback.

I did not win. In fact, I may not have beaten anyone else that day. But as I walked over to get on my bicycle and ride home, Mr. Corcoran, one of the teachers officiating the event, stopped me. He handed me a yellow place-kicking tee. This, he said, was for being such a good sport.

I don't know if he simply felt sorry for me or if I had actually done something that smacked of good sportsmanship. I do know this: The fact that I still remember that yellow kicking tee and the message behind it validates the significance of the moment. Someone taught me early in my life that sports were about more than beating the other guy. And once that seed was planted, it grew in me with gusto.

Twenty-five years later, I still believe we too often worship at the scoreboard altar. But I remain convinced that the athletic arena, as a microcosm of life, makes for a rich classroom. Sometimes the lessons are warm and fuzzy, sometimes hard and cold. Always they offer insight to fathers and sons willing to be students, even if we may have to repeat a few classes along the way.

One of the most important lessons a father can teach his son about sports is that for all the good they offer, they will ultimately fail us if we let them become our gods. In 1988, I was sitting in a park in Bellevue, Washington, reading a *Sports Illustrated* magazine while my two sons played on the swings. The deeper I got into a particular article, the more aghast I became.

It was about Marv Marinovich, an ex-pro football player who had decided to raise his infant son, Todd, with one goal in mind: to make him a superstar quarterback in the NFL. He conducted actual ball-tossing drills in his son's crib. He put his son on a regimented practice schedule as a pre-schooler. He brought in sports psychologists to work with him as a grade-schooler. He brought in a nutritionist who put Todd on a diet that wouldn't allow even an occasional hamburger. Run. Run. Run. Throw. Throw. Throw. Push. Push. Push. But Marv got the results he sought: Todd won a full scholarship to the University of Southern California, Marv's alma mater.

Once home from the park, I fired off a letter to *Sports Illustrated*, which was published three weeks later:

> I wish Todd the best of luck at USC. But should he not become the best quarterback ever to throw the ball, or not even make it to the Rose Bowl, I hope Marv won't see him as a failed laboratory experiment. Instead, I hope he's big enough to say, "I'm proud of you anyway, son." And perhaps take him out for just one Big Mac.

Todd became a star at USC. He was drafted by the Oakland Raiders and became a starting NFL quarterback, realizing his father's dream. But this morning, my clock radio woke me with a story quite similar to stories I've heard ever since the younger Marinovich went to college: He once again had been arrested on drug charges. And he's now out of the NFL—a has-been before the age of 30.

I ache for Todd Marinovich and, to some degree, for a father who thought he was doing what was best for his son. I ache for Todd because he grew up without something that a lot of kids are growing up without these days: a childhood. The joy of play. The innocence of imagination. The freedom to create and not be controlled. Instead, he grew up as robo-quarterback, a son whose worth to his father was measured in touchdown passes.

I ache for his father because in trying so desperately to raise a winner and to live through that winner's achievements, both father and son wound up losing.

At some point, every parent of talented kids must make a decision: What price success? How far will we go to help our children succeed? What are we willing to sacrifice in order for them to make it on the next echelon? Will we give up the family's summer vacations so he can play year-round basketball? In essence, what price glory?

Early on, my wife and I made a decision that we would not bet childhoods and family vacations and thousands of dollars a year on our sons becoming athletic superstars. The equation was simple: The risks outweighed the perceived rewards.

Did we want them to succeed in sports? Unquestionably. And we've been willing to allow sports to become a fairly significant part of our lives. But when it came time to play in this elite league or try out for that special team or attend this swanky camp, we said no. And the boys never once objected.

Why? Because they were too busy wearing base paths into our back lawn with whiffle-ball games that lasted long into the summer nights. (They, of course, had rigged stadium lighting.) They were too busy exploring the rocky fingers of Sparks Lake. Too busy making video movies. Playing make-believe Rose

Bowls on a rug we lined upstairs with masking tape yard lines.

In short, too busy having childhoods.

As they grew up, they found success on basketball courts and baseball diamonds and golf courses, too. Not the kind of success Marv Marinovich was seeking, though. As a sophomore, my oldest son earned the seventh and final spot on his high school's junior varsity golf team; when he told me the news, I got choked up.

Fathers don't normally grow misty-eyed when their son makes the last spot on the JV squad. But I had learned that success is based not solely on how far you've gotten, but on how far you've come. For the previous two years, as his buddies grew like watered weeds, Ryan had not. And, in a sense, he had been left behind in athletics because of his small size. So for him to try out for a team against players he didn't know at a school with 2000 students in a sport in which he had never before played competitively was a courageous step. And for him to make that team was a validation of himself and the hard work he had invested—the kind of validation he hadn't experienced in years.

It taught him to risk failure. To believe. To try even harder. Unlike much of his competition, Ryan is a blue-collar golfer. We haven't belonged to a country club where kids can play unlimited golf. Instead, Ryan went to work at a public course, shagging range balls until 10 and 11 P.M. in Oregon's infamous winter rains for minimum wage, free golf, and all the balls he could hit. He built his swing not by taking private lessons, but by overhearing the golf pros give lessons as he picked up empty range buckets, and by going out back and chipping balls, which outnumber plants in our garden about 100 to one.

Meanwhile, Jason's successes have come mainly in baseball, the most notable of which occurred in a single moment last summer. In the last three years, I doubt Jason has ever taken the field or the basketball court when he wasn't the smallest player on either team. Last summer, his lack of height was all the more noticeable because he was a seventh-grader playing in a seventh/eighth-grade league.

A fire-armed pitcher—more than a foot taller than my 4-foot-9 son—blazed a fastball right down the pike. I'm not sure Jason even saw the ball. Strike one. The second pitch scorched across the plate for a called strike two. The third pitch, unintentionally I'm sure, came right at Jason. He turned to avoid being hit and fell to the ground. His bat went flying. His helmet bounced off. The ball seemed to have skimmed his shoulder.

"Take your base," said the umpire.

Standing in the third-base coach's box, I was happy just seeing Jason alive, much less getting a free base. But now he was saying something to the umpire. What was going on?

"It didn't hit me," Jason said to the ump.

"Take your base, son," said the ump.

Our fans were likely thinking the same thing I was thinking: *Take your base, son. You've been wounded, soldier; your war's over. You're going home....*

"But honest, it didn't hit me," Jason pleaded.

The umpire looked at Jason and out to the infield ump, who just shrugged. "OK," said the ump, "the count is one-and-two."

Should I intervene? Make him take his base? Jason was already digging in his cleats in the batter's box. I mentally shrugged and headed back to the coach's box.

The towering pitcher rocked and *fired*. A bullet right down the middle—the kind of pitch that would send the kid to the dugout. Instead, Jason ripped the ball into left-center for a stand-up double. Our crowd roared. The manager of the team in the field was standing a few feet behind me. He had no idea that the kid on second base was my son. He spit out his sunflower seeds and slowly shook his head.

"Man," he said, "you gotta love that."

My sons and I no longer play together as much as we once did. Times have changed. The Backyard Baseball Association scoreboard I made for the boys sits on the side of the house, warped from too many rainy Oregon winters. Our ball bins are full of flat balls. Mike Riley, my grade school pal, is the new head coach at Oregon State, where his father was once an assistant.

But here's the return on investing in our kids at eye level: Our photo albums are full of rich memories: the year Sally and I lost to the boys in a Turkey Bowl football game, and the score was broadcast on a Seattle TV station's Turkey Bowl scoreboard ("Jason and Ryan, 35; Mom and Dad, 28"). The Birthday Olympics—one event which included making a putt while skate boarding. And, of course, the countless knee-football games, which I remember every time I feel pain in my knees.

I would almost always let the boys win. And they would almost always feel rotten and cry if they lost. But what those games made me feel more than anything else was important to my sons.

You gotta love that.

Fall

A time of change

*The only sense that is common in the long run,
is the sense of change—and we all
instinctively avoid it.*

—E.B. White

For fathers and sons, autumn is a season of transition. A bridge from the warmth of summer to the harsher days of winter. In autumn, sons transform from dependent to independent. Fathers, at least in the eyes of their sons, transform from super-heroes to humanoids with no ear for *real* music.

If summer is relatively simple, autumn grows complex. Summer meanders along like a lazy river, each bend bringing more of the same. But in autumn, fathers and sons encounter the riffles of changing expectations, the rapids of distorted communication, sometimes the falls of polarized values.

In autumn, handshakes and high fives replace bed-time kisses. You call home, and a stranger with a deep voice answers; it is, you realize, your 16-year-old son.

It is a time when things you took for granted can no longer be taken for granted. It is a time to cinch up that life jacket and hold tightly to the raft's oars, realizing that you're in for a tumultuous ride that will thrill you and scare you.

For above all, autumn is a time of change.

WAKE-UP
CALL

I was sitting in a bathtub full of moldy sheetrock when my 13-year-old son asked the question. "Can you take me golfing sometime?" he said.

I had a bathroom to remodel. It was fall, and the forecast for the next week was for 100 percent chance of Oregon's liquid sunshine. I wanted to say no. "Sure," I said. "What did you have in mind?"

"Well, maybe you could, like, pick up Jared and me after school on Friday and take us out to Oakway."

"Sounds good."

Friday came. The showers continued. Looking out the window, moldy sheetrock seemed the saner choice. But at the appointed hour, I changed from home-improvement garb to rain-protection garb and loaded the boys' clubs and mine in the back of the car. In front of the school, Ryan and Jared piled in. Ryan looked at me with a perplexed expression.

"What's with the golf hat, Dad?" he said.

It was, I thought, a silly question, like asking a scuba diver what's with the swim fins.

"Well, I thought we were going to play some golf."

A peculiar pause ensued, like a phone line temporarily gone dead.

"Uh, you're going, *too?*" he asked.

Suddenly, it struck me like a three-iron to my gut: I hadn't been invited.

Thirteen years of parenting flashed before my eyes. The birth. The diapers. The late-night feedings. Helping with homework. Building forts. Fixing bikes. Going to games. Going camping. Going everywhere together—my son and I.

Now I hadn't been invited. This was it. This was the end of our relationship as I had always known it. This was "Adios, Old Man, thanks for the memories but I'm old enough to swing my own clubs now, so go back to your rocking chair and crossword puzzles and—oh yeah—here's a half-off coupon for your next bottle of Geritol."

All these memories sped by in about two seconds, leaving me about three seconds to respond before Ryan would get suspicious and think I had actually *expected* to be playing golf with him and his friend.

I had to say something. I wanted to say this: *How could you do this to me? Throw me overboard like unused crab bait?* We had always been a team. But this was abandonment. Adult abuse.

This was Lewis turning to Clark in 1805 and saying: "Later, Bill. I can make it the rest of the way to Oregon without you." John Glenn radioing Mission Control to say, thanks, but he could take it from here. Simon bailing out on Garfunkel during "Bridge Over Troubled Water."

Why did it all have to change?

Enough of this mind-wandering. I needed to level with him. I needed to express how hurt I was. Share my gut-level feelings. Muster all the courage I could find, bite the bullet, and spill my soul.

So I said, "Me? Play? Naw. You know I'm up to my ears in that remodel project."

We drove on in silence for a few moments. "So, how are

you planning to pay for this?" I asked, my wounded ego reaching for the dagger.

"Uh, could you loan me seven dollars?"

Oh, I get it. He doesn't want *me*, but he'll gladly take my *money*.

"No problem," I said.

I dropped him and Jared off, wished them luck, and headed for home. My son was on his own now. Nobody there to tell him how to fade a five-iron, how to play that tricky downhiller, how to hit the sand shot. And what if there's lightning? What about hypothermia? A runaway golf cart? A band of militant gophers? He's so small. Who would take care of him?

There I was, alone, driving away from him. Not just for now. Forever. This was it. The bond was broken. Life would never be the same.

I walked in the door. "What are you doing home?" my wife asked.

I knew it would sound like some 13-year-old who was the only one in the gang not invited to the slumber party, but maintaining my immature demur, I said it anyway.

"I wasn't *invited*," I replied, with a trace of snottiness.

Another one of those peculiar pauses ensued. Then my wife laughed. Out loud. At first I was hurt. Then I, too, laughed, the situation suddenly becoming so much clearer.

I went back to the bathroom remodel and began realizing that this is what life is all about: change. This is what fathers and sons must ultimately do: change. This is what I've been preparing him for since he first looked at me and screamed in terror: not to play golf without me, but to take on the world without me. With his own set of clubs. His own game plan. His own faith.

God was remodeling my son. Adding some space here. Putting in a new feature there. In short, allowing him to become more than he could ever be if I continued to hover over him. Just like when I was a kid and, at Ryan's age, I would sling my plaid golf bag over my shoulder and ride my bike five miles across town to play golf at a small public course called Marysville that I imagined as Augusta National.

I remember how grown-up I felt, walking into that dark clubhouse, the smoke rising from the poker game off to the left, and proudly pluncking down my two dollars for nine holes. Would I have wanted my father there with me that day? Naw. A boy's gotta do what a boy's gotta do: grow up.

I went back to the bathroom remodel project. A few hours later, I heard Ryan walk in the front door. I heard him complain to his mother that his putts wouldn't drop, that his drives were slicing, and that the course was like a lake. He sounded like someone I knew. His tennis shoes squeaked with water as I heard him walk back to where I was working on the bathroom.

"Dad," he said, dripping on the floor, "my game stinks. Can you take me golfing sometime? I need some help."

I wanted to hug him. Rev my radial-arm saw in celebration. Shout: "I'm still needed!" I wanted to tell God, "Thanks for letting me be part of this kid's remodel job."

Instead, I got one of those serious-dad looks on my face and stoically said, "Sure, Ry, anytime."

UNCOOL

The Oregon-Washington football rivalry is not a matter of life and death. No, people in the Northwest will tell you it's much more important than that. And so it was that on an October afternoon in 1995, Duck fans were strutting their feathers far and wide after the University of Oregon's 24-22 win in Seattle.

After the game, my son Ryan, then 16, left for work, but I stayed and listened to a local radio station's call-in show. The University of Oregon callers were justifiably proud. But pride turned into gloating, and gloating into Husky bashing, and Husky bashing into individual-player bashing. In particular, the host and callers were razzing the Husky field goal kicker, who had missed two last-minute attempts to win the game.

They were sarcastically thanking him over the air. Saying he flat out choked. Saying how glad they were that it wasn't *them* walking into his fraternity house that night.

Enough. Before I knew it, I had climbed on my moral high horse, cellular phone in hand, probably spurred on by some subliminal childhood message from my mother. When a team was getting blitzed to smithereens, she would always say something like: "Those players have mothers, too. I feel sorry for them."

"You're on the air," the host said.

I introduced myself, said I was thrilled to see the Ducks win, but thought that some of the callers had stooped too low in riddling the Husky kicker.

"Sorry, Larry," said the host, "but I disagree."

"It's Bob, not Larry."

The host, apparently not a fan of 1 Peter 3:9 ("Do not repay evil with evil or insult with insult"), said Duck fans had a right to be obnoxious since Husky fans have been obnoxious when the University of Washington wins, which is most of the time.

"But," I said, thinking of a line I had used over the years with my youth teams, "we've got to win with class and lose with class. The stuff I've heard isn't very classy. What if that kicker were your—"

"Sorry, Larry Bob," said the host. "Got another caller. 'Bye."

Larry Bob? Just like that, the soapbox was pulled out from under me. But I shrugged it off and went on with my day. When Ryan got home from work that night, I asked if he had listened to the call-in show. He had, on his car radio while en route to his job at a golf driving range.

"Did anyone on there sound familiar?" I asked.

He shook his head no and headed up the stairs. Then suddenly he froze on the fourth step. "Wait a minute. Hold on. Dad, that wasn't—I mean, no. Tell me that wasn't—you weren't that *Larry Bob* guy, were you?"

I started laughing.

"I don't *believe* it," he said, turning and burying his face in his hands. "We've just beaten the Huskies, everyone's enjoying the win, and here comes this guy on the radio to spoil the party."

I laughed harder.

"Honestly," he said, "when I heard that guy, I said to myself: 'Get a *life*, buddy.' I'm like, 'I gotta tell Dad about this guy. He's a total *loser*.'"

In every father-son relationship, moments like these announce to a father something he never thought he would hear: In his son's eyes, he is totally uncool. Such moments might happen over a few weeks, a few months, even a few years. But they're marked by a not-so-subtle suggestion that the father who was once Mr. Everything has become McFly of *Back to the Future* fame: a wimp, a goody-goody two-shoes, a nerd.

A major reason for this inevitable father-son chasm is that, as fathers, we always want to be our son's hero. And frankly, because it's so simple being a hero to your children when they're young, it's hard when you grow older and realize you're not.

When my youngest son was in kindergarten, every week during the school year was dedicated to a different letter of the alphabet. And to help the students learn those letters, the teachers asked them to bring something each week that began with that particular letter.

When it was Jason's turn on the letter B, he was particularly imaginative.

"Dad," he said the night before his assigned day, "I need your help. Could you come to school with me tomorrow?"

At first I didn't understand. Was he fearful of something? Did he need an assistant for some kind of trick or experiment? Then he explained his plan, and I gladly complied. The next day, after the rest of his classmates had stood up and displayed items such as balloons, basketballs, and ballet slippers, he turned to me and said to his curious classmates: "Here is my B word. This is my dad, Bob."

It was one of the proudest moments of my life. But then, those were the days when you could make your son proud simply by standing up with a name tag on that said: "Hello. My name is Bob."

Times change.

Within a few years of that incident, my worth as a father was suddenly based on performances. Not any performances. But performances that would be scrutinized by my son's teachers, his classmates, and his classmates' parents. I'm referring, of course, to my personal *Nightmares on Elm Street:* school science fairs.

These were to be the first chinks in my fatherhood armor. For at least four generations, Welch men have been arts and letters guys, or prank guys, or outdoor guys, but not science guys. Honestly, you could run me through a weekend seminar on how a light bulb works, and I would still flunk the final exam.

Compounding my science-fair phobia was that, for much of my boys' elementary school years, we lived in Bellevue, Washington, backyard to Boeing, the largest maker of jet airplanes on the planet, and Microsoft, the largest maker of software on the planet.

In other words, the parental competition was brutal. There was my son, standing beside our "How Electricity Works" demonstration, which consisted of a dry-cell battery, two wires, and a little flashlight bulb. To our left was some kid whose dad was a Boeing engineer, with a demonstration something like "The 747 Simulator: Virtual Flight for a Virtual Generation"—a display so impressive that you all but expected a gift shop at the end of it.

To our right, the kid with the Microsoft Mom was showcasing something like self-designed software that, in minutes, could take an entire class's lunch order, give each child a calorie-and-protein count of what they had ordered, and spit out a bar chart contrasting the popularity of, say, pizza to tacos.

Once, just being my son's father made me a hero. You could even do stupid stuff and not endanger your hero status. After buying hundreds of baseball cards for the boys over a few years' time, I decided to keep them organized by hanging them on a strip of molding lined with dozens of nails. This, of course, required me to punch holes in each of the cards, which I later learned was akin to, say, affixing the Mona Lisa to a museum wall with a staple gun. It didn't do much for the cards' resale value. But unlike today, my kids were no smarter than I was, and so this atrocity didn't even rate a blip on their Dad-as-nerd radar screens.

Then your kids grow up and reach a point where they're not as easily fooled or as easily impressed. The problem isn't that you've lost your superpowers; the problem is your kids get smart enough to realize what you've known all along: You never *had* superpowers.

When I was 33, I wrote a magazine cover piece on what had become of all my heroes from a 1967 college football team that I had idolized as a teenager. What I found shocked me: Many of the players had wound up living fairly troubled lives. What had changed so much wasn't their lives but my perspective.

As a 13-year-old, my requirement for being a hero was simple: Wear an orange-and-black football uniform that said "Oregon State" on it. The players could have been car thieves and thugs for all I cared. As long as they wore the uniform. Twenty years later, my standards were higher. It wasn't enough that they had all played on this special team; I wanted them to have made a difference in the world, become good husbands and fathers. And at the very least, I wanted them to have avoided the pitfalls of addictions, which many of them had not.

Once, we were heroes to our kids just because we wore the Dad uniform. But times change.

I remember when Ryan, as a high school sophomore, first beat me in 18 holes of golf. I felt good about it. I told the congregation about it during morning announcements at church. I put together a special fake newspaper article on the milestone. I made good on an earlier promise and rewarded him with a new putter.

Even so, something—a different strain of that same pride?—wants the kid to know that I'm not going to concede the next match on the first tee. Wants him to know that I can still catch the long ball in street football.

When I was young, I never felt a need to compete against my father because he wasn't particularly competitive, nor did he enjoy sports other than fishing. But as I became a teenager, I did consider him uncool. And that realization suggests I shouldn't look at my current situation with code-blue fright.

Though not much of a golfer, my father played a few rounds after I got interested in the sport in junior high. Once we were walking off a par-3 green when suddenly a wayward ball from the foursome behind us bounced off my dad's head. Though he had to be carted back to the pro shop, he was OK. But I remember thinking, with my decidedly narrow 15-year-old perspective: Of course it would be *my* father who would get hit by a golf ball. Other people's dads belonged to the country club, knew you didn't mix plaids with stripes, and didn't get hit in the head with golf balls.

It was also uncool, I felt, that my father seemed particularly sullen and worried during my teen years. And that, in a sense, his jobs didn't require him to use much of the creativity I knew he had. My father had an amazingly artistic eye; like his father, he could draw beautifully. He also could take wonderful nature photographs. And yet his jobs required little of that artistry.

He sold cameras, made educational films, and worst of all, took group shots at fraternity and sorority dances at the local university. At some subconscious level, I probably thought he had sold out, hadn't followed his dreams, had squandered his gifts. Sometimes, I would tag along to help carry his equipment to those dances, and I remember feeling hurt that these drunken college kids accorded my father so little respect. (Why I blamed him for that, I'm not sure.)

Ultimately, what made me better understand him were two things: my growing up and his dying. "When I was a boy of 14," Mark Twain once wrote, "my father was so ignorant. I could hardly stand to have the Old Man around. But when I got to be 21, I was astonished at how much he had learned in seven years."

Once I had a broader perspective, I could see my father so much more clearly. And once he died, I finally took the time to understand why he might have been the way he was.

Rummaging through some of what he left behind, I came across an advertisement for his *Trout in the High Country* movie that he had made himself. And I realized that He *did* have a dream. He *did* use his creativity. This movie was it. For years, I've looked back on that movie as if it were just family trivia, a hobby, some cheesy flick that interrupted my precious sleep when he would be trying to dub the sound track at night when everyone was in bed, and he would make a mistake, yell, and have to start over. But now I realize that film meant as much to him as one of my books means to me; it was an extension of himself. It was his dream. And when that dream didn't fly, he became the wounded warrior that I became when one of my book or magazine proposals was rejected.

Perspective. That's what this father-son stuff is all about. It's about treating people the way we would want to be treated, the kind of Golden Rule thinking that seldom makes a teenager's priority list.

If I had been more sensitive, I might have been thankful that my father even made the effort to play golf with me and less critical of him for being in the way of an errant golf ball. I might have been more thankful that my father willingly weathered those partying college students. Because the money he earned from those dances ultimately allowed me to earn a journalism degree so I didn't have to spend my life taking pictures of drunken college students. I never remember my father complaining about his jobs; his generation accepted hard work as simply paying their fatherly dues. My generation expects more—too much more.

If I had been more sensitive, I might have stopped to consider that, in the fall of my junior year, the college research department my father made films for was cut, and he lost his job. No wonder he was sullen and worried; he was wondering how he was going to take care of me, my mom, and my sister, who had just started college.

Looking back, I've realized that my father was struggling during my teenage years. And it wasn't as if he was going to share those hurts with me every morning while driving me to school—any more than I was going to suddenly blurt out over my Frosted Flakes: "Dad, I'm scared about growing up."

We each harbored our own hurts and didn't do much to share those hurts with one another. I wish we had talked more, but we didn't. I would like to think I communicate better with my sons, but I wonder. I wonder if they see me the same way I saw my father.

If I'm uncool in my sons' eyes, it's probably because they think I try too hard to analyze every situation I see instead of simply going with the flow. They would prefer that I just cheer on their high school basketball team, instead of assessing the sportsmanship of every player. That I would just relax and be late for church instead of giving them a lecture on how being late tells a speaker or teacher or pastor, "You're not important." That I would just bash the Huskies like everyone else instead of phoning in like some sort of ethics cop.

They're right, of course. I could stand to lighten up. Our greatest strengths, when taken to extremes, become our greatest weaknesses; one of my greatest weaknesses is getting so passionate about something that I expect the entire world to share my passion—preferably right this moment.

Still, I don't think the solution to this uncoolness is checking my values at the door until the boys are old enough to understand my motives. In fact, I think the solution has less to do with understanding what fathers and sons need from each other than understanding what God wants from us both.

He wants fathers and sons to care as much about each other as they do about themselves.

He wants us to love each other not based on our performances, but unconditionally—just because we *are*.

Finally, if I understand His Word correctly, He wants fathers to understand a truth that some might find surprising: As a father, being cool is not your ultimate goal. Being holy is. Being godly is. And doing your best to raise godly sons is.

When my sons are older and look back at their father, I hope they remember someone who cared. In the meantime, the Larry-Bob story is getting great mileage and, just tonight while we were watching family videos, someone wondered whatever happened to the infamous school science fair project I made.

It is stored in the shed. If uncoolness is genetic, as I suspect it is, the grandchildren might need that light bulb and battery someday.

TURNING 16

Dear Ryan,

Tomorrow you turn 16. In a week, it's likely you will be driving our car all by yourself. I can only describe my feelings on the eve of this milestone birthday as mixed.

On one hand, I am heartened to see what an awesomely cool young man you're turning out to be—the kind of kid any father would be proud to have, but who I have been blessed to call "son."

On the other hand, I would be less than honest if I didn't tell you that I am also concerned. Not that you'll somehow let me down; for starters, you weren't placed on this earth to live up to my expectations. Not that I'll somehow lose you as you bid farewell to boyhood; I sense that you and I will always be friends. In fact, I'll be surprised if, when I'm 60 and you're 35, I won't be trying my darnedest to outdrive you on every hole.

What I'm concerned about is simply that, in the next few years, you will be making the kind of decisions that will very likely have a huge impact on the rest of your life. Next week, for example, you will most likely earn the right to drive a motor vehicle. How you choose to drive that motor vehicle will have a huge impact on your life because cars are the biggest killers of teenagers.

In the next few years, you will be deciding where you're going to college, what kind of profession you might want to pursue, where you want to live, and perhaps whom you might want to marry, if you decide to marry. Above all, the cement will be drying as to who you want to *be*. What you want to stand for.

Given the gravity of such decisions, please indulge your old man as he steps up to the pulpit and offers you a little advice.

1. Make God and people—not money, position, and things—your top priority. First, it's biblical; in Matthew 22:37-39, Jesus says our priorities are to love God and love those around us. Second, they are the only things that last. Fame is fleeting. Quick, who won the 1993 Super Bowl? (I can't remember either.) Money comes and goes. Today's CEO is tomorrow's fired CEO.

What people want is security and to be loved, and yet they look for it in all the wrong places. It's found in a relationship with Christ, who loved me and you enough to die in our place. Who, in a world in which people's love for each other is usually dependent on getting something in return, loves us unconditionally. Who allows us the privilege, if we simply trust in Him, to live forever.

And security and love are found in family. At times, Ryan, I must admit, I envy the freedom of some men who play more than a hundred rounds of golf a year and can seemingly take off whenever they please. But my favorite part of every day is walking into my home knowing that I have three people who love me passionately. I have found no greater joy in life than being a husband and father.

2. Stop to smell the roses. You and I had a wonderful time at Tokatee Golf Course last Sunday. But did you notice

what happened because we played so fast? We didn't get a chance to notice the way the mountains reflected on the pond on the 11th hole or listen to the ducks waddling behind the 14th green or smell the woods after the heavy rains. Sports are wonderful, but don't get so wrapped up in the competition that you miss the ride.

3. Keep your promises. We live in a world built on mistrust. We sue each other right and left. We promise to love and honor each other for a lifetime, then get divorced when things don't go our way. We make bold political promises to get reelected, then forget those promises once we're elected. The Bible says, let your yes mean yes and your no mean no. Walk the talk.

4. Put the toilet seat down. 'Nuff said.

5. Persevere. Life is tough. Period. The key is not creating a wrinkle-free life; that's impossible. The key is overcoming the obstacles that get in the way. It's like a round of golf. The key isn't hitting every shot perfectly; it won't happen. The key is overcoming your bad shots with good shots. Persevere. Never give up. On God. In sports. In school. In marriage. Anything.

6. Express yourself. That can, I know, mean a lot of things. It might mean writing a letter to the editor if you feel an injustice has occurred. But I'm thinking of it more in the sense of letting people around you—and God—know how you feel about them. We somehow assume people know we care about them. But I'm always amazed at the power of a simple note, a card, a small present. People need constant reminders that they're significant.

7. Remember that God molds our character through discomfort. Through challenge. It's the same way an athlete gets better. He or she has to find resistance: a lap to run, weights to lift, balls to hit. Sure, you can be comfortable by not facing any resistance, by not sweating or climbing or risking. But you will never grow as an individual. You will get bored. And you will spend the rest of your life watching soap operas.

8. Choose your friends wisely. In the next few years, your friends will influence you perhaps as much as anything else in this world. Choose people who value what you value, who care for you as a person, not because you wear the right clothes or say the right things or know the right people. God has blessed Mom and me with friends who, I'm convinced, would come to our rescue in our darkest hours. Choose friends who would come to your rescue in such times. (P.S. It wouldn't hurt if they had a ski boat, either.)

9. Let your actions speak louder than your words. People recognize a hypocrite right away. But they appreciate someone who actually lives his spoken ideals. Why? Because it's so rare.

10. Remember your roots. You're part of a family. Part of something bigger than you are. Take pride in that. In the family tree of which you're a part, do what you can to leave behind a sturdy branch.

11. Laugh. Often and loud. Do something off-the-wall on occasion, as long as it doesn't hurt someone. Laughter can heal. It can soften a hardened heart. But use it carefully.

12. Keep sex where God intended it to be: in a marriage relationship. Our society has cheapened sex to where it's just something two people do for a good time—the bedroom equivalent of grabbing a bite to eat or going bowling. Sex, by God's design, is a beautiful expression of love between a man and a woman who have committed to each other for life.

13. Learn to discern right from wrong. In the next few years, you'll be bombarded with advice—subtle and overt—from teachers, peers, the media, etc. But something isn't necessarily true because someone important says it is, or even because Mom or I say it is. Or because 52 percent of the people vote a certain way. Truth is what God says it is.

14. Never make the first or third out at third base. Chances are, if that runner were back at second, he would score just as easily from second on a hit as he would from third.

15. Don't be afraid to say you're sorry. Or you blew it. It is perhaps the hardest thing in the world to do, because it

involves something we, as humans, cling to so ferociously: pride. But it softens the hardest heart. And leads to reconciliation in a relationship like nothing else can.

16. Pray. God is the most powerful resource we have. But He's nothing if we don't communicate with Him. Don't be pious when you pray. Just be honest. God looks at your heart.

17. Read. Read. Read. And don't just read books you know you'll agree with; read other books, too, because they will sharpen your faith and help you understand why some people are the way they are, even if you don't agree with them.

18. Humility is a greater virtue than pride. I don't care what the TV commercials say.

19. Here's one I picked up from your Grandmother Welch: If you're making fun of a little ol' lady crossing the street real slowly, just remember: She's someone's grandmother.

20. Never forget how much your mother and I love you. And will always love you. Nothing—absolutely nothing you do—will ever change that.

Thanks for allowing me to share some thoughts, even if they might have seemed a bit on the preachy side. And thank you for the privilege of being your dad.

I'm so very proud of you.

Love, Dad

STAYING IN
TOUCH

My sons and I were winding our way over the Coast Range en route to a spring weekend at the beach, and I was in one of those Friday afternoon feel-good moods. A tough week of work was behind me. My wife and wave-watching lay ahead. The sun, something we Oregonians hadn't seen since roughly October, was slipping low in the western sky.

I felt like talking. Asking questions. Taking advantage of my captive audience and communicating, the three of us engrossed in a virtual father-son festival of spontaneous verbal exchange, sharing the depths of our souls while the mile markers zinged past.

"Highlight of your senior year, Ry."

"Huh?"

"What would you say has been the highlight of your senior year so far?"

"Beats me."

"Low light?"

He shrugged.

"Best all-time comedy movie, Jas."

"I dunno."

"Best teacher?"

He rolled his eyes and muttered a name I couldn't hear.

This wasn't quite the level of soul-baring I had in mind. But I figured they probably just wanted more zip on these verbal pitches; what's the challenge of hitting slow, straight stuff?

I fired a slider, low and away—an ethical decision I needed to make at work regarding a newspaper story that had the potential to seriously damage someone's career. Do we run it? Why? Why not?

They both responded with solid singles. But I wanted more. I gripped the threads for a change-up.

"OK, here's one," I said. "What is it about me that bugs you guys?"

Both watched this one all the way into the catcher's glove. Not even a wisecracking, "Only one?"

I regripped and threw a similar pitch. "No, really, tell me something I could improve on. Something that I do as a dad that you don't like."

Ball two.

"Hey, here's your chance to be honest with me about ways that I've hurt you," I said. "Things that I can change. So come on: Name one of my weaknesses as a father."

Ryan's bat met this one squarely. "I guess sometimes when you're mad about something—maybe it's something at work—you take it out on us, as if we were the problem when we weren't."

I could hear Dodger announcer Vin Scully in the broadcast booth: "Ryan Welch rips a hard liner right back at the pitcher. Oooh, that's a stinger. He's slow getting up."

But I recovered. "You're right," I said. "If you'd asked me the same question about myself, that's probably what I would have said. I need to work on that.

"So, Jason, how about you? What bugs you?"

He didn't say anything.

"Come on, there must be something."

"Well," he said, after a long pause, "I guess there is one thing."

"What?"

"The way you ask so many questions," he said.

•   •   •

It didn't used to be this way. When the boys were small, we communicated all the time. They would share a virtual play-by-play of everything they had done all day.

Before going to bed, we would talk about all sorts of things. I would give the boys an opportunity to ask me questions—"anything in the world"—and they would fire pitch after pitch at me. Easy pitches. ("Do police officers have homes?") Difficult pitches. ("Where did I come from?") All sorts of pitches. ("Do fish go to church?")

Then, as we entered the father-son season of fall—also known as the teen years—communication changed. I'm driving the boys to school and realize that, other than sports talk, we don't say much. Or the dinner-table conversation is decidedly lopsided.

"So, how was school?" I ask.

"Fine."

"Why was it so fine?"

Shrugged shoulders.

"On a scale—"

"Dad, please don't do that 'On a scale of 1 to 10, how would you rate your day' stuff."

"Fine," I say, my feelings not at all hurt. "On a scale of 1 to 25, how would—"

"Dad, can we just eat?"

I've been thinking a lot about communication with my kids lately and have developed a theory about what happens in those teen years. But to explain my theory, I'll need to shift my metaphor from America's pastime to space travel because this is a problem too vast to fit onto a baseball diamond.

If you saw the movie *Apollo 13*, perhaps you remember the part where the astronauts are desperately trying to jury-rig a way to get back home. Meanwhile, as they orbit the far side of the moon, communication with Mission Control on earth is temporarily interrupted.

At some point, most fathers and their teenage or near-teen sons go through that same kind of crisis. Dad sits at Mission Control, trying to explain what son-in-hormonal-orbit needs to do to get back to earth. Son, meanwhile, is trying to jury-rig his own system to get back—assuming he, uh, wants to get back. Meanwhile, as Son wings his way to the far side of the moon, communication with Mission Control temporarily shuts down.

Uh, Houston, we have a problem. . . .

It's a worrisome time for sons, even though they would never admit it; "I'm fine...just leave me alone."

My amateur psychology, coupled with the NASA theme, suggests it's all a matter of gravity. Son is trying desperately to break free of parental gravity into that wonderful adolescent atmosphere that's free of all responsibilities, particularly room-cleaning and being-home-by-11. His motto: "To infinity and beyond..."

Now in his mid-life years, Dad, meanwhile, has just been told by the flight board that he's been permanently reassigned to Mission Control. After years of rocketing around the earth as a space cowboy, he has a desk job. He's a middle-aged guy who, when reading the newspaper, notices an increasing number of ages in the obituaries are just a few years beyond his, and an increasing number of business-promotion ages are considerably below his. The closest he'll come to defying gravity anymore will be riding the Matterhorn at Disneyland. His motto: "Is this all there is?"

Boom. Two people, each struggling with who they've been, who they are, and who they're destined to be. A teenage son is all about becoming more than he's been. He's driving for the first time. He's dating for the first time. He's

Super-gluing a pair of your favorite work sneakers to a 1″ x 8″ board to make an impromptu snow board for the first time.

But a middle-age father is all about trying to remain all that he's been. He's a step slow on the basketball court (OK, three). He's ten pounds heavy on the scale (OK, 15). And, most likely, he's facing what Christian author Robert Hicks in his book *The Masculine Journey,* calls "the wounded warrior" stage of life. Maybe he's taken a risk and lost. Maybe he had dreams that haven't come true. Maybe he looks at himself in the mirror and sees the face of his father, and to some degree finds that scary.

You used to be Isaiah 40:31 come-to-life, able to "run and not grow weary." Suddenly, your doctor is saying: "You're getting a little soft in the belly, Bob." You used to be invulnerable. Suddenly, a nurse in the exam room hands you a survey that says "Rate Your Urinary Performance."

And you're thinking: *When did it come to this?*

Meanwhile, your son is running and not growing weary. In fact, he's going to school, playing 18 holes of golf, going to work, playing basketball with his girlfriend, going to hear a Christian rap group at a coffeehouse at 9 P.M., then over to so-and-sos to watch a video, and after that, rolling in about midnight.

Making a metaphorical shift from outer space to the Himalayas—my, we do get around, don't we? — father and son may be climbing the same mountain, but they're at far different points in the journey. And when they occasionally rendezvous at base camps along the way—also known as home—Junior is more concerned about stocking up on supplies—also known as food and money—than relaxing with Pop and discussing the intricacies of the climb. Or asking how to set an ice pick. Or sharing his fear of falling.

But here's what I'm learning: Instead of lamenting that my question-and-answer session en route to the beach didn't pan out like I had hoped, I need to be thankful that amid the gravel I found a nugget of gold: Without hurting my feelings, my son was able to share something about me that hurt him. If I'm Proverbs 12:15 wise—"The way of a fool seems right to him, but a wise man listens to advice"—I can use that to help be a better father.

Instead of lamenting that he's climbing a southwest ridge and I'm on a northwest wall, I need to appreciate that we're climbing a mountain together. And for all the navel-gazing I do in regard to growing older, I need to remember that just because I'm not a space cowboy anymore doesn't mean I have to give up on dreams; like my son, God wants me to become more of who He made me to be. The two of us, father and son, may have more in common than we think.

Instead of lamenting what makes my sons and me different, I need to remember what we have in common, and use those places, interests, and activities as opportunities to communicate.

For the last couple of years, I've read some of the same novels Ryan has been required to read in English classes; originally, I did it so we could discuss the books together and help him write better essays. But the unexpected side benefit has been a chance for us to share thoughts on the books' themes.

For example, in *All Quiet on the Western Front*, a German soldier writes of finding himself in a foxhole with a dying enemy soldier, and how, for the first time, he realizes the soldier was a man, just like him, with a wife and child. The segment led to an interesting discussion about how easy it is to pigeonhole people who don't share our values or lifestyles as the enemy when, in fact, we're bound by our humanity—and fighting a war not of our choosing.

Now, let's cut closer to the bone. Instead of lamenting that my sons don't talk with me enough, I need to ask a question that hurts: Do I listen to my sons enough? Not just listen in the sense of processing, but do I "hear between the lines"? Hurting teenagers rarely serve up their feelings on silver platters; more often, it's a Manager's Surprise. Do I do enough to hear that hurt? To decipher that hidden message? To discover that cry for help?

Instead of lamenting how seldom we seem to communicate, I need to remember that communication is a mysterious thing. Just because my son doesn't respond to something I've said doesn't mean he didn't hear it. Nor does it mean it didn't make an impact on him. Over the years, I've left lots of notes for my sons; seldom do they acknowledge receiving those notes. But acknowledgment is not necessary for a thought or feeling to have been transferred.

Instead of lamenting that my sons are so seldom vulnerable with me, I need to ask, How often am I vulnerable with them? Humbling himself and being real—even sharing hurts of his own—may be the most important thing a father can do to improve communication with his sons; ironically, it also may be the most difficult.

But it breaks down walls. Why? Because when one person is willing to be vulnerable, it gives permission for the other to be vulnerable. So often we hesitate to say something because we fear we won't say it the right way. Say it anyway; the right motive is infinitely more important than the right words.

A month ago, the basketball team at Ryan's high school made it into the state basketball tournament, which is played in Portland (110 miles north of Eugene, where we live). For a variety of reasons, it became an emotional week for our family. Going to and from games, we were ships passing in the night, Ryan riding to games with friends, Sally and I taking our youngest son and others.

Suddenly, Ryan asked a question that hit Sally and me hard: Could he drive a handful of friends to one of the late-night games? The moment he asked, I envisioned a Corvair smashing into a freeway overpass, which is what happened to four kids in my hometown who were killed after a state tournament in the late sixties. Ryan pressed us; he's 17, he said. He's responsible. He'll drive carefully. But I'm back in 1969 at the A&W on Western Avenue, thinking about a friend of mine whose girlfriend died in the crash.

One of the hardest things about parenting is letting go. After much prayer and hand-wringing, we allowed Ryan to drive. It was a long night, waiting for him to arrive. We figured he would be home between midnight and 12:30 A.M. He arrived at 1 A.M.

As the week wore on, we were all getting tired. The good news: The team was doing well. They made it into the finals. In the championship game, our team built a nine-point lead with only about five minutes left. Watching Ryan and the student body going wild down below, I suddenly realized what a pleasant surprise this could be: My son's school could be the state basketball champs. What a nice ending to 12 years of lower education. He was going nuts with his classmates—a green-and-white mass of wild and crazy innocence.

But about the time I was thinking all this, an opponent hit a three-point shot, then another, and still another. The lead evaporated. Our guys panicked a bit. Before I knew it, the game was over. We had lost. As the awards were handed out, our players sat on the bench, faces buried in their hands, crying. They had had the dream-come-true in their hands, then let it slip away. Our students just stood there, stunned. Ryan was crushed. On the two-hour drive home, he hardly said a word.

The next day after church, we were eating lunch in a restaurant when Ryan and I got into an argument about why we had lost the game. I blamed it on one player in particular. Ryan felt that was unfair. We went back and forth. Sally and Jason sided with Ryan—or at least it looked that way to me. I felt like the defender on a three-on-one fast break. Make that a 12-year-old defender, based on how immaturely I was acting. We drove home. Nobody spoke.

I went out to chop wood. I was drained, physically tired, and suffering from an emotional hangover. But for me, chopping wood sometimes does more than create kindling; it splits open those knotty logs from that woodpile of life that I so often avoid. The kind of logs Gospel-writer Matthew described when he said, "You hypocrite, first take the plank out of your own eye, and then you will see clearly to remove the speck from your brother's eye."

As I split each piece of oak, I started to contemplate what had just happened. Why I had become so emotional. And why, with each swing of the maul, I was turning to emotional mush. Suddenly, Ryan walked by, en route to his car.

"I need to tell you something," I said, without even thinking.

He waited. The words were stuck. Sometimes the mind tells the mouth to move but it will not.

"I'm . . . sorry . . . I got . . . mad," I said, the words coming like cubes from a stubborn ice machine. "I was wrong. I've been thinking about why I got so emotional, and I think it's because last night, as I sat there and we had that nine-point lead, I looked down at you and I was so happy for you. You were pumped. And then suddenly, the game was over, and I looked at you and I could see how hurt you and the players and students were. It was almost disbelief—to be so close and then to lose. And so I guess I blamed that player because, in a sense, I felt he robbed you of that dream.

"It wasn't his fault. It wasn't anyone's fault. I just wanted them to win it so badly—for you."

At this point the dam crumbled and emotions flowed. I hugged Ry and he hugged me, and I felt like a blubbering fool but wouldn't trade the moment for anything.

Because in a world with war, a billion starving people, and nagging racial strife, a basketball game is fairly trivial stuff. But a father and son reconciling in tears. That's important stuff.

That's communication. Sometimes it comes in the form of words. Sometimes in the form of actions. Sometimes it comes adorned in tattered trimmings, a sweaty father dropping a splitting maul and hugging his son.

But when it comes, it's like the crackling of that radio aboard Apollo 13 after hours of silence. It's a welcome relief that, amid a journey into an unknown universe, a journey in which communication sometimes goes dead, we are still in touch with each other.

MY MOUNT EVEREST

While putting up the outside Christmas lights today in a typical Oregon drizzle, I found myself lost in introspection. That's not particularly strange for me; traditions like this often trigger memories, which get me considering all those big-life thoughts and, suddenly, when I should be thinking about which extension cord goes to which outlet, I'm thinking instead about my place as a tiny human speck in God's endless universe.

Being alone helps, too. My wife doesn't do holiday exteriors. And my sons, now 17 and 14, no longer treat the decorating of the house as the sacred Christmas ritual they once did: As I toiled at midday, my oldest was off to the golf course to hit balls, and I assumed my youngest was still asleep, having ignored my encouragement to practice his basketball dribbling in preparation for an upcoming tryout.

But beyond the traditions and the aloneness, it's also the height that triggers this occasional soul-searching. When standing on a roof, you're afforded a rare glimpse of life around you: blocks and blocks of houses and backyards and people and dogs and cars. And this seldom-seen perspective gently invites you to ask yourself philosophical questions like: What part do I play in this vast suburban theater? Who are all these fellow actors, most of whom I don't even know beyond a name on a mailbox? And finally: When did my next-door neighbor dismantle his aluminum storage shed? Where does he store his lawn mower now?

Which then leads to a profound spiritual question: Are we to love our neighbor even if he ruined the weed whacker of ours he borrowed? Even if the unauthorized "adjustments" he made to our rototiller left it leaking more oil than the Exxon Valdez?

All of which is to suggest that I was already in a fairly contemplative mood when, while on the extension ladder, I placed one hand on the gutter and swung myself to the top of a fence, a slightly dangerous move that, when successfully completed, left me smugly pleased until—well, until I thought of Jon Krakauer.

Jon Krakauer is a high school classmate of mine who has climbed Mount Everest. Whose book *Into Thin Air* (Villard)—about surviving the climb in 1996 that killed nine others—has summited the *New York Times* bestseller list. Who, in 1997, has been on all the major television news shows and in all the major newspapers and magazines.

Imagine, I thought, the highest point on earth. Nearly six miles high, roughly the same height that jetliners travel. Pretty heady stuff for a guy like me, whose biggest challenge on this December morning was standing ten feet up on a ladder, trying to correctly align gutter clips so my bulbs would be even.

But there's more: Krakauer makes his living flying around the world as a freelance writer, doing adventure stories for *Outside* magazine. He can make the English language roll over, beg, and fetch perfect metaphorical phrases on command. And, what's more, when I broke up with my girlfriend in the winter of 1972, it was Jon Krakauer with whom she rode off into the sunset.

So there I had been, in my pre-Krakauer thoughts, a middle-aged father of two thinking I was doing something pretty darn noble. As if Hugh Downs were going to glance at his side monitor at the end of "20/20" Friday night and say: "Ted Koppel, tell us about tonight's Nightline topic" and Ted were going to say: "Hugh, Barbara—tonight we take you to Eugene, Oregon, where Bob Welch, for the twenty-second straight Christmas season, has put up his outdoor display lights for his admiring family without his wife, Sally, having to call 911."

Now, as the drizzle turned to a full downpour, Everest was on my mind. Blizzards. Oxygen masks. Ice picks.

I secured my old water-ski rope to a 4" x 4" post holding up the back porch and wrapped the rope around me, then climbed to the peak and down the other side of the wet roof.

(This made me think briefly of a story I had heard about a guy who had taken a similar safety precaution. Only he had secured his line to the rear bumper of his Suburban—a solid anchor, he figured, for going down the far side of a pitched roof. But probably not the best choice if your wife suddenly decides she needs to run a quick errand in the Suburban, which this guy's wife did. As I understand it, the guy survived and, even more astonishingly, the marriage survived. However, ever since that day, the man has scaled back his outdoor Christmas display. It now consists of one small wreath on the front door.)

When my boys were small and would see me at the peak of the gabled roof, the looks in their eyes said, "My father is standing on top of the world. He is the most amazing man on the planet." Now, my youngest, instead of practicing his dribbling as I had gently suggested, was probably waking to my footsteps above him and thinking: "Do you *have* to do this while I'm trying to sleep?"

As I tacked up strings of lights, the ghost of Krakauer continued to haunt me. I had climbed life's conventional routes: college 40 miles from home, marriage, kids, church on Sundays, and vacations at the beach, our once-in-a-lifetime adventure being a trip around the West in a 1989 station wagon. (You're not going to see that one nudging out "Heliskiing the

Himalayas" or "Sea Kayaking the Fiji Islands" for the cover of *Outside* magazine.) I had started work the day after graduation, stayed in the same business, and invested in only conservative mutual funds.

Meanwhile, after high school, Krakauer had hitchhiked back to a private school in Massachusetts, where students planned their own curriculum. As a freelance writer, his office has been the glaciers of Mount McKinley, Antarctica, the Alps. Eventually, he got married. He and his wife—not my ex-girlfriend, by the way—chose to not have children, believing they would interfere with the couple's adventurous lifestyle.

Let's face it. Jon Krakauer was Indiana Jones of *Raiders of the Lost Ark* fame, in search of the lost ark of the covenant. And I was Clark Griswold of *Christmas Vacation* fame, in search of a three-way adapter so strings 8 and 9 could mate with extension cord C.

My fingers grew numb in the driving rainstorm. After about four hours of work, I began wondering why I do this every year. Does anybody really care whether we have Christmas lights?

And worse: *If I were to slip, how long would it take before they would find my crumpled body and haul me off to the hospital?* It wasn't a particularly noble thought, I admit, but when you start looking up at people who have climbed higher than you, sometimes you lose perspective on life altogether and think ignoble thoughts.

Finally, the rain let up. I was straddling the highest peak on the house, thinking what it must be like to straddle a narrow ridge 29,028 feet atop Mount Everest, when I heard it: the voice of my youngest, who had come outside with a basketball in his hand.

"Hey, Dad," he said. "Be careful up there. Wouldn't want you to fall."

He then smiled, opened the gate of the back fence, and began dribbling down the street, zigzagging back and forth, pretending he was in a game, trying to break the full court pressure. Just as I had shown him.

I watched him until he turned the corner and then thought: *He doesn't really care that I've never been to the top of Mount Everest. What he cares about is that I don't fall 20 feet off my roof and break my neck.*

With God's blessing, I've somehow helped create this little human being who wants me to stay safe. Who somehow needs me. Who even occasionally heeds my advice.

As I stood on the peak of the house, nobody but me realized the amazing fact that I—Bob Welch, Christmas light decorator extraordinaire—was at that very moment on top of the world.

SEIZING THE
MOMENT

In the cool of the August morning, two golfers blow on their cupped hands to ward off the chill. They stand on the tee and look ahead toward their target, lost somewhere in the darkness of 6 A.M. It's an arrow-straight hole until a slight dogleg right at the end. Water—actually lots of water—left. Trees and beach grass right.

And lots of sand. Lots and lots and lots of sand.

You see, this golf hole stretches seven miles long. It was created by me and my 16-year-old son by sticking a soup can in the sand about 12,320 yards north of my grandfather's beach cabin on the Oregon coast, then driving back to play our one-hole course.

Par 72, we figure.

This sea monster makes the 948-yard sixth at Australia's Kooland Island Golf Course—the longest hole in the world, according to Guinness—look smelt-esque by comparison. But this challenge is more than man versus monster. It's also father versus son, as it's been since the knee football games began nearly 16 years ago.

Ryan steps to the first—and only—tee. Like a young gymnast, he fears nothing. *Thwack.* He hits one straight down the middle.

When did he get so strong?

I step to the tee, like a 41-year-old man who fears nearly everything, particularly a water trap on my left—the Pacific Ocean—that spans 70 million square miles and covers one third of the earth's surface. When God made the sea and saw that it was good, He obviously wasn't taking into consideration my hook on an oceanside course.

But I, too, hit straight and long. I may be aging, but I refuse to go gently into the good night.

We're off into the morning mist. The gullery is decidedly uninterested, most of the feathery fans too busy ripping the guts from washed-ashore crabs to pay much attention to us.

That's fine; we're not here for glory. On the low side of the split-level green of life, we're here for the same reason one man in an office will shoot a crumpled memo into a wastebasket and another man will slap it away as if he were David Robinson: We're competition freaks who do crazy things involving sports.

But on the high side of the split-level green, we're here because the father part of this twosome is increasingly aware that time and tide wait for no man.

He sees a son who, Lord and admissions directors willing, will be off to college in a couple of years and will probably be doing more mature things, like painting his entire upper body with school colors for home football games.

This father-son stuff won't go on forever, this dad has realized lately. It's autumn, but winter awaits like storm clouds over the Coast Range. He's heard all those sermons about parents being the bows and children being the arrows, and he knows the archer must soon let go. Plus, he's read the late golf guru Harvey Penick's book that encourages golfers to "Take dead aim." The axiom, the father has come to understand, goes beyond the golf course to life itself.

What's more, the same father determined months ago that a minus-tide on this particular morning of the family vacation would stretch the fairway to its optimum width. Three hundred yards is a gloriously wide margin of error for someone like myself who once shattered a car windshield with a wild hook.

And because of the early-morning tee time, the father reasoned, few people would be soulfully walking the beach, thinking deep thoughts about moving to the Oregon coast to write novels when, just as they are accepting the Pulitzer prize for fiction, reality hits them right between the eyes—in the form of a Titleist 2.

Down the windless beach we head, two waves at different points in our journeys to shore. I see Ryan as a silhouette against the eastern sky and think, *When did he get to be so tall?*

We each carry but one club: a driver, for maximum distance. I hit the ball farther in the air, but Ryan takes better advantage of the hard sand with line drives that hit and roll forever. At Big Creek, three miles after teeing off, he has a full stroke on me, 26 to 27.

We each wear a fanny pack filled with extra golf balls that unmask my spoken bravado. Ryan has packed three extra balls. Me? Twelve.

As the charcoal sky turns to light blue then salmon pink, the match remains tight. The sun bursts through the trees at the four-mile mark, turning the surf to a frothy white. The smoke from a state campground flavors the cool air.

We play Rules of Golf with Beach Alterations: Every shot may be placed on a wooden tee, of which we've brought many. But anything in the water—be it ocean, tide pool, creek, or lagoon—cannot be removed without a one-stroke penalty. Seaweed, logs, and dead gulls are not considered loose impediments and, thus, cannot be moved.

Hit, walk. Hit, walk. The journey continues. Past motels. Past cabins. Past deep-thinking walkers who stroll the fairway as if they were on a beach.

We make small talk. In the months to come, as Ryan grows more independent, there will be time for deeper things; for now, both of us still yawning, it is enough that we comment on flocks of sandpipers, rib each other relentlessly about who will win, and compare hunger pains, which our Big Hunk candy bars soon fix.

Then it happens. Near Yaquina John Point, with a mile to go, disaster strikes Ryan. It is the long-distance golfer's equivalent of a sailor's mast breaking: His last tee snaps in half. He must now hit off the hard-pan sand with a driver—a difficult task.

Half of me wants to console him and loan him a tee; half of me wants to exploit this advantage for all it's worth. Being the sensitive mid-life father I am, I smile like the Grinch who stole Christmas and push the thrusters to Full Exploit. This is, after all, a kid who loves to beat me at everything from arm wrestling to Yahtzee. Who only occasionally loans me *my* pickup. Who chides me for thinking PFR is a medical acronym, not a Christian band.

I must cling to my dignity any way I can get it. Ryan doesn't grouse; he simply buckles down and does his best.

When did he get so mature?

A hundred yards out, with the seaweed-flag now in sight, we are dead even. Father and son. Sixty-two shots apiece.

After we each hit four more shots, Ryan is 12 feet and I am 3 feet from the hole. The pressure mounts.

Ryan lines up his putt, steps over the ball, strokes and—misses. He looks to the sky in agony before tapping in for a 4-under-par 68.

So it comes to this: After seven miles and 16 years, I make this simple putt to remain the family's beach golf king.

I stand over the ball that I teed off with four hours earlier. (Amazingly, Ryan and I have each used only one, though the sand has all but worn off the dimples.)

All is quiet. A few crabbers watch curiously from their boats in nearby Alsea Bay. The air is still.

I stroke the putt. As if pulled by a soup-can magnet, the ball rolls straight for the cup, for the jaws of victory, for the gentle reminder to my worthy young foe that, in the sea of life, I'm more than just some 40-something flounder, that I'm—suddenly, inexplicably, the putt veers left like a sickly crab and dies two feet away from the hole.

Huh?

We tie. But after a handshake and a maple bar, I realize that we have come a long way, father and son—much farther than seven miles. We have shared a sunrise, something we've rarely done. We have made a memory that may be told around beach fires for years to come: "You know I purposely missed that last putt."

"No way, Dad."

"Sure. You didn't think I actually wanted to beat you, did you?"

Above all, we have taken dead aim and hit life's real target which, in God's eyes, has nothing to do with swinging a golf club and everything to do with seizing a moment.

No, I realize as the incoming tide erases our footsteps on the beach, we don't tie.

We win.

THE COCAINE KID:
PART I

In the summer of 1982, as a 12-year-old, Danny Edland hit .744 for his Little League baseball team in Redmond, Washington. Not .700. Not .750. But .744. When you're a father and you're trying desperately to see your son succeed in a way that you did not, you remember your son's successes with great precision. And Norm Edland was that father.

He could tell you, with great accuracy, how many touchdown passes Danny had thrown, how many boxing matches he had won, how many words he had spelled right in getting to the spelling-bee finals.

He wanted Danny to be everything he had not been. And to do that he figured he needed to be everything his own father had not been. His father had been an alcoholic who had no time or interest in Norm.

"As a youth," Norm once wrote to me, "I received no love or support from my father of any kind. I decided that, as an adult, I would totally love and support the efforts of my children. I can honestly say I have never heard of a child who received more personal love and support than Danny did."

As a journalist, I've reported thousands of stories in the last 20 years. The subjects of those stories generally come and go, as if I were nothing more than an assembly-line worker who placed a tiny piece of notoriety on each of these human widgets. Until that moment, I had never seen these people before. Then, finished with my part of the job, I would send them on down the line, knowing I would probably never see them again.

But Norm and Danny Edland were an unforgettable exception. I have followed the tragedy-stained trail of their lives now for 12 years, even though I have moved from Washington to Oregon and am now an editor and not a reporter.

In 1986, as a columnist at the *Journal-American* newspaper in Bellevue, Washington, I got a call one morning from a man in his early 40s. He wanted to know if I was interested in writing about a 15-year-old boy, the son of two well-heeled, have-it-all professionals whose large suburban house featured a Porsche and a Ferrari in the garage.

"What's so interesting about this kid?" I asked.

"Well," said the man. "He's a cocaine dealer." The man thought a column by me about this kid might deter some teenagers from getting into drugs.

"And how do you know him?" I asked.

There was a pause on the other end of the line. "Because," the man said, "he is my son."

Usually, the father-son shift from summer to winter is a gradual one, but for Norm Edland and his son Danny, it was not. Instead, autumn arrived with an ambulance racing to an emergency room.

The previous night, while high on drugs, Danny had tried to kill himself. "Do you know what it's like to see your son—the same son you coached in Little League a few years ago—lying in a hospital emergency room after trying to commit suicide?"

Norm invited me to meet with him and Danny. That afternoon, I opened the door to the American Dream and found the 250,000 dollar house was a facade, a front, a Hollywood prop. Inside, I found only pain and broken promises. Behind the opulence, I found only emptiness.

I found a father with a type-A personality and a high-powered sales job that kept him on the road most of the time, peddling high-end electronics. A father who defined his success in dollars—105,000 dollars a year. A father who wanted so desperately to erase the past that, in essence, when Danny stepped to the plate, Norm saw himself in that batter's box. And he had a single mission: to prove to himself that he could hit whatever pitch his dead father might throw, even the high-zingers aimed at the head.

I saw a boy with vacant eyes, unable to sleep because of cocaine use, eating ice cream out of a gallon carton. I heard him mumble about making 10,000 dollars over the summer, selling to some 300 customers. About freebasing 500 dollars' worth himself one night. About his interest in compiling a nest egg so he could invest in stocks.

And why had it come to this? Norm blamed the judicial system. If the punishment for dealing drugs had been stiffer, his son would never gotten into the business. Over and over, he lashed out at The System. The System that failed his son—meaning The System that failed Norm himself.

Could Norm, who was either on the road or shouting instructions from behind the backstop, have played a part in this? Why wasn't he around more for his son in the in-between times, in the times when nobody's keeping score and a 15-year-old just needs to talk?

"Why wasn't I around?" he said. "I'll tell you why: Because I'm an American. I make money. Big money."

I watched Norm point to a row of his son's sports trophies. His favorite one was the one of Danny in a football uniform standing next to him. "I decided to be to him what I always wanted my dad to be like to me," said Norm. "That's why I coached and umpired."

His son became obsessed with being the best. "He wanted to be in fanatical condition," said Norm. "Watching TV, he'd do 500 to 1000 sit-ups or push-ups, perhaps because he was always afraid of losing."

He dealt drugs with the same enthusiasm. The boy had always had an entrepreneurial bent—paper routes, lawn jobs, and the like. "He still has his first nickel," Norm said.

With each example of Danny's obsession to be the best, to earn more, to be Number 1, Norm's voice dripped with disgust. It was as if he didn't see the big picture, didn't see the similarities between his making 105,000 dollars a year and Danny making 10,000 dollars a summer, between selling electronics and selling cocaine. Didn't see the similarities between Norm Edland and a teenage son who, in some circles, was known as the Cocaine Kid.

On one side of the room sat a father who, because of the deficiencies in his past, had lived his life through his son. On the other side of the room sat a son who, because of the fear-of-losing lessons from his dad, had turned out just like his father.

Two people who, deep down inside, wanted to be each other. Two blind men trying to inch their way along a trail notched into a canyon, desperately holding on to one another. But if the journey already seemed treacherous, it was only beginning.

The winds of winter hadn't even begun to blow.

Winter

A time of letting go

An easy thing, O power Divine,
To thank Thee for these gifts of Thine,
For summer's sunshine, winter's snow,
For hearts that kindle, thoughts that glow;
But when shall I attain to this—
To thank Thee for the things I miss?

—Thomas Wentworth Higginson

Winter arrives. In the natural world, it is the season of death and dormancy, the quiet culmination of all those autumn changes. Once-vibrant trees turn bare. High-mountain lakes freeze in submission to the season. And darkness outduels light.

So it is in the father-son world. Winter is the season of separation. Of physical departure. Of emotional distances. And sometimes of death itself.

We turn inward. We turn less to experience and more to contemplation. In winter, memories magnify themselves in the minds of fathers who miss their sons. And haunt those burdened with regret.

Beauty abounds in winter, but it is a more subtle beauty that can be missed unless one puts the season in perspective,—realizing, for example, that it is the harsh rain and snow of February that will nourish the rhododendrons come spring.

It is a time of stark awareness of all the seasons that have passed before. It is a time when we more naturally look back to what was than ahead to what may be.

It is a time of letting go.

THE COCAINE KID: PART II

After spending that August afternoon with Norm and Danny Edland, I returned to the office and wrote my column about the 15-year-old cocaine dealer and his father. Nothing I wrote for that newspaper in the seven years I was there triggered so much response. It would seem that Norm's hope—that a column might deter some other kids from using drugs—might come to fruition.

But confronting his cocaine dealing in print didn't deter Danny Edland. Shortly after the article appeared, he was arrested for possession. "I'd gone from hopes and dreams to watching my son be led away in handcuffs," said Norm.

Danny went to a local drug rehab center, but was asked to leave when dealers started pestering him. Norm and his wife then chose to send him to a nonvoluntary rehab center in another state. "That was the toughest day of my life," said Norm. "He just kept crying and holding his dog."

The center did nothing to help Danny. Meanwhile, though, Norm took a key step toward healing this broken family: He admitted his own alcoholism and went for treatment at a ranch in central Washington.

Danny got busted again for dealing marijuana and was sentenced to 15 days in a juvenile detention center. Finally, all of it became too much: the arrests, the blackouts, and the diet of only ice cream, licorice, and orange pop. "I was dying slowly," he said, looking back.

Said Norm: "He came to me and said, 'Dad, I'm tired of being tired.'"

Together, the two went to the ranch for treatment and came back like new people. They sorted through their lives and found a father who wanted to be everything to his son that his alcoholic father had not been to him. And because of that, a father who perhaps pushed too hard to be a six-figure breadwinner, and pushed too hard to make his son the all-American athlete.

The son's rebellion was the switch from sports to drugs—an arena in which he secretly "competed" against his father. "I thought I was better than him," said Danny. "I mean, I made more money in a weekend then he could make in a month. I emotionally destroyed him."

Finally, reconciliation. The two bought motorcycles and started riding together. They took walks on the beach. Went to movies. "Whatever hasn't killed this family has made it stronger," said Danny.

For his father's birthday, Danny wrote his father a poem:

> Thank you for helping me
> through the years
> and crying with me
> when I shed my tears
>
> You have meant so much
> to me each day
> sorry it took
> so long to say.

Taking a new job at the *Register-Guard* newspaper in Eugene, Oregon, I occasionally thought about Norm and Danny

Edland over the years. But I didn't hear a word about them for a long time.

Then one day a letter arrived from Norm. My heart sank. Danny had relapsed. After their reconciliation, he had attained his real estate license; one of his bosses told Norm, "He's a natural—the smartest kid I've seen in 30 years in the business."

He was making good money. But why settle for a .500 batting average when you can bear down and hit .744? After he completed a sophisticated land deal that earned him 3000 dollars, Danny put much of it up his nose in the form of cocaine. Norm was numb. Addicts, they say, only get better after they hit bottom. "Danny seems to have no reasonable concept of that term," he wrote.

His son then wrapped a car around a telephone pole in an accident that an officer said could easily have killed Danny and his passenger. Two weeks later, in a borrowed car, he rammed a parked car, which hit a house, causing 30,000 dollars in damages. He fled the scene and was arrested for hit-and-run, and for driving while intoxicated.

"Spinning totally out of control, he continued on his little rampage as the courts absolutely refused to take any action," wrote Norm. "His lawyer kept him out of jail."

At least for a while. When Danny started dealing again, an elaborate sting operation busted him. He was sentenced to 33 months in prison. "He was so totally out of control that I begged the court to 'get him off of the streets before he kills himself or someone else,'" wrote Norm.

He was sentenced to a maximum-security prison in Shelton, Washington. "The trophies you saw gathering dust on the shelf in our upstairs recreation room are stored in a box in a spare room in the house we now live in," Norm wrote.

Then he philosophized about what he would do differently if he could start over again.

If I knew then what I know now, I most definitely would have lived my life in a different manner. The nine Porsches and the Ferrari are wonderful for the ego, but they mean obviously nothing as it relates to what is real in life. Danny has been the source of my greatest joy and also my deepest despair. I cheered him as a youth and wept, in total frustration, as I watched him being led away in handcuffs or sentenced to prison.

Once, while visiting him in prison (where he sat in a concrete room and we were separated by thick glass and had to speak to each other on a telephone), I said, "Danny (and I had tears in my eyes as I spoke to him, just like I have tears in my eyes as I write this), what could I have done differently? What did I do wrong?"

He answered, "Dad, it wasn't you. It was just the booze and the drugs."

I don't believe what he said, Bob. I'll go to my grave knowing that simple love and total support aren't enough.

At the end of the letter, he congratulated me on the release of *More to Life Than Having It All*—my former paper had done a story on my book—and asked if I would write to Danny in jail and encourage him.

Before responding, I looked back at the articles I had written about him. What could I possibly say to this kid? How do you reach someone who seemingly doesn't want to be reached? I thought and prayed, then wrote this:

Dear Danny,

You probably don't even remember me. I'm the reporter who did the stories on you for the *Journal-American*. But I'm not writing you as a reporter, I'm writing you as another human being who, like you, is trying to make his way through this oft-tangled world.

I want to offer you a few thoughts, not because I'm older than you and should necessarily know more. Not because I get high by moralizing. But because I honestly care about you as a person.

First, perhaps you think you're in prison and everybody outside those bars is free. Wrong. We all live in prisons of sorts. Some people's prison is a $500,000 house that they are a slave to because the payments are so high. Some people's prison is a six-pack of beer, a needle, a line of coke. Some people's prison is their own ego; because of it, they can't see themselves for who they really are and, thus, can't change the way they need to. Some people's prison is work, others a hobby; it's whatever controls us.

Second, perhaps you think nobody cares about you. Wrong. I would assume lots of people genuinely care about what happens to Danny Edland. And I know, in particular, one is your father. Danny, I know he has never been the perfect father, but I'm not sure I've met a man who cares so much about his son.

Finally, perhaps you think what's gone on in your past is unforgivable. Wrong. I know your parents are more concerned about your future than your past. None of us has to go through life burdened by our failures; if so, we'd all be miserable, for all of us have failed.

But here's the deal: I'm convinced that whether we're in prison or in the penthouse suite of the world's finest hotel, we are absolutely doomed if we try to make it through life without connecting with our Creator. The older I get, the more I'm convinced not that I'm right and everyone else is wrong, but that God is right and people's ways are wrong.

Oh, how we struggle to disprove that theory. We so desperately want to prove that we can make it on our own. (Hey, it's the American way. We've been raised believing there's no such thing as a free lunch.) So we try to buy our fulfillment. We try to get it by outdoing the other guy at work or on the ball field or in the drug ring. We throw ourselves into causes. We do it by trying to lord power over other people. Some who profess to be Christians do it by cloaking themselves in pious righteousness.

If all this doesn't work, we turn to the man-made life rings. We seek therapy. We meditate. We take weekend self-esteem workshops. We read tarot cards. We chant. We hang upside down. The problem is this: All such answers are man-made. The therapist is just a person, like you or me. Sometimes we seek justice in the courts; but the judge is a person, like you or me. Some of us believe if we can just get the right leaders into office or pass the right law, life will work. But who fills those positions and who makes those laws? Fallible human beings, like you and me. Still others, rely on education. The problem? Academics, like the radio talk-show hosts, are adept at asking life's questions but inept at answering them.

So what is the answer? Religion? No. Religion, as people like Jimmy Swaggert and Jim Bakker have proven, is no answer because, again, it's comprised of fallible human beings—some of whom deceive to line their pockets. Church? No. Certain churches can bring us closer to the answers, but punching in and out of a building once a week is no panacea for life's struggles.

The answer, I've come to believe, is a relationship with the one who created us: God Himself. And He provided a bridge for us—everyone, regardless of position, pasts, race, sex, age, whatever—to come to Him, through Christ His Son. The world, Danny, is not divided into Christians and non-Christians, good people and bad; good and evil coexist in every human heart. No, the world is divided into people who are willing to humble themselves before God and people who are not.

I'm not in the business of laying guilt trips on people. But I would be less than honest if, to encourage you, I simply said, "keep a stiff upper lip" or "hang in there" or "get professional help." I believe there is power in God, and it's a waste to not tap that power.

Remember those three assumptions I made about you? God is the answer in each case.

First, He's the one who can free us, whether we're in jail or out of jail. "I am the way, and the truth and the life. No one comes to the Father but through me" (John 14:6). And "If you hold to my teaching, you are really my disciples. Then you will know the truth, and the truth will set you free" (John 8:32).

Second, He cares about you like no other. You are infinitely valuable to Him, and your value is not dependent on your faithfulness to Him or on your past. He loves you despite your sins. "Look at the birds of the air; they do not sow or reap or store away in barns, and yet your heavenly Father feeds them. Are you not much more valuable than they?" (Matthew 6:26).

And finally, God will forgive you for anything you've done in the past. That doesn't mean you still won't have to pay consequences for those misdeeds, nor does it mean you can keep on doing wrong. But He'll wipe your slate clean. "If we confess our sins, he is faithful and just and will forgive us our sins and purify us from all unrighteousness" (1 John 1:9).

I want to leave you with the hope of one man who offered some memorable words back in the '60s. He said,

> Godliness with contentment is great gain. For we brought nothing into the world, and we can take nothing out of it. But if we have food and clothing, we will be content with that. People who want to get rich fall into temptation and a trap and into many foolish and harmful desires that plunge men into ruin and destruction. For the love of money is a root of all kinds of evil. Some people, eager for money, have wandered from the faith and pierced themselves with many griefs. But you, man of God, flee from all this, and pursue righteousness, godliness, faith, love, endurance, and gentleness. Fight the good fight of the faith.

Fine, you say, it's easy for someone to pontificate while sitting in some ivory tower instead of behind bars.

Danny, I've got news for you: That statement was written in A.D. 65 by the Apostle Paul.

While in prison.

Your friend, Bob

I sent him the letter, along with a copy of *More To Life Than Having It All*, which suggests that contentment is ultimately found in relationships—with God and others—not in materialism. Danny wrote back, thanked me for the letter and book, and said, "I have always been such a bad person that even if I can change a little, I will never be deserving of that kind of happiness."

At Christmas, he wrote and said that for the first time he noticed "the true meaning of the word *Christmas*." He also said that he was being released soon, wished "good cheer" to my "wonderful family," and signed his letter "With love." He had gotten married and had a daughter.

The response buoyed my hopes. Then, a few months later, came a letter from a woman back in Washington, where I had first written about Danny. She had clipped a news story from the Bellevue paper. The headline jolted me:

Four Eastsiders collared in coke bust

The story itself was more stunning than the headline. Because along with Danny Edland and two friends, the fourth person arrested was someone I never dreamed I would see in a drug bust: Norman Edland, Danny's father. The man who had stuck with his son for a decade, trying to pull him out of the quicksand of cocaine, had slipped into the bog himself.

Released on bail, the two were to be sentenced together. But in the months leading up to the sentencing, Norm told Danny that he didn't want to face it. Danny told his father he must.

On the night before the two were to be sentenced, Norm called his son and, out of the blue, told him that nothing in the world meant as much to him as Danny and Danny's new baby daughter, then hung up. Danny sat in silence, thinking about what he could do to save his father. But at that point, nobody could have done anything for Norm Edland.

Later, the autopsy report would show he died from a self-inflicted gunshot wound—a single shot to the head.

ON BECOMING
A MAN

A good friend's son turned 21, and I was invited to a party in the young man's honor. It was like no other party I've been to. About a dozen other men, ranging in age from about 30 to 65, showed up, each of them bringing not food, drink, or even presents, but a single item requested by my friend: a symbol of an event in our lives that helped us make the transition from boys to men.

This was new for us, particularly since some of us joked that we were still waiting to make such a transition ourselves. We all showed up a bit mystified, as if guests at one of those TV murder-mystery dinners in which someone keels over during dessert and the next two hours are spent figuring out who dunnit. We slammed down a few delivered pizzas and mugs of root-beer floats—nobody died from either—and chatted a bit nervously. Then my friend called the event to order.

"You're all probably wondering what you're doing here," he said, as we settled into the family room. "Let me explain: To me, turning 21 represents a step into manhood. You've all made that step. And each of you has been invited because at one point or another, Bryan has expressed respect for you."

We all looked around at each other, with "Who, me?" looks on our faces. We were just a bunch of ordinary guys: a contractor, a software engineer, a journalist, a youth pastor, an accountant, a graphic designer, and a few other professions that don't normally elicit VIP thoughts.

"So I'd like to go around the circle and have each of you share an event that helped you become a man. My hope is that someday Bryan will look back at this event and remember some of what you shared."

What followed was an intriguing two hours of men sharing from their hearts in a way I've seldom seen men share. One man gave Bryan an old silver dollar and talked about his parents teaching him the importance of working hard for an honest dollar; for him, becoming a man meant integrity.

Another man gave Bryan a copy of Psalm 73, and told a story about sitting in an Alaska motel room, realizing that he needed to quit his job because his business partner had cajoled him into operating unethically; for him, becoming a man meant staying true to God's Word.

Still another, named Kevin, gave him a bicycle seat and told him about living in Korea, and about a house boy named Mr. Kim who promised to fashion the man a bicycle seat to replace one lost in a move. On the day he was to meet Mr. Kim, Kevin forgot. Mr. Kim waited three hours in the rain. For Kevin, becoming a man meant doing something he had failed to do on this day: being responsible to others, regardless of their social position in life.

As the afternoon wore on and the stories unfolded, I was reminded that manhood had less to do with age than with enlightenment. With commitment. With repentance.

Like my friend, I believe that the age of 21 carries with it at least a cultural endorsement of manhood, a sort of Good Housekeeping seal of approval for those coming of age. And yet if we're honest with ourselves, we would admit that America bestows the 21-year-old with a rather hollow honor: in most states, the right to drink alcohol.

Are we to believe that the essence of manhood is found in the freedom to drink? As the stories came forth, it reaffirmed my thought that manhood had much more to do with responsibilities than with rights. Manhood isn't found in a bottle. It's found in the hearts of men, in the form of such attributes as courage, humility, and vulnerability.

One man gave Bryan a miniature soccer ball, and told of the seemingly insignificant times that, as a basketball coach, he had reached out to players from dysfunctional families—players like rudderless ships whose lives were blown with the capricious winds of drugs, crime, and apathy. He told about how years later some of those players would thank him for having an impact on their lives. For him, becoming a man meant loving the unlovable.

Another man gave him a handball. He told of being obsessed with being the best, and how finally he came to the realization that while winning on the scoreboard, he was losing in the sight of men, who took one look at his Rambo-esque approach to handball and wondered: Where, in this robotic man, dwelt the peace of Christ? For him, becoming a man meant humbling himself.

The afternoon wound to an end. Finally, only one man was left to share: Bryan's father, Rick. He pulled out a small box and began telling a story about Bryan's step-grandfather, who was a communications specialist at Pearl Harbor during World War II.

When the surprise attack by the Japanese began on December 7, 1941, he began running from the barracks to the communications headquarters to tell the world what was happening. En route, fragments from a bomb shattered his leg and ripped into the side of his head. He struggled into the headquarters, turned on the radio equipment, and told of the attack.

His message, said Rick, was the first word to the rest of the island and to the States. "When someone found him, they thought he was dead—he eventually had to have a steel plate in his head—but because of what he did, many lives were saved."

For Rick, becoming a man meant a willingness to put one's life on the line for others.

He opened the box and presented his step-grandfather's Purple Heart medal to his son Bryan. And there, on a Sunday afternoon in a family room surrounded by a dozen men and plates of pizza crust, a father and son hugged.

Man to man.

ROSES

O
n January 2, 1995, my two sons and I watched our beloved University of Oregon Ducks play Penn State in the Rose Bowl. Thanks to a friend with connections, we sat on the 45-yard line: Section C. Row 27. Seats 14, 15, and 16.

From the Goodyear Blimp we were just three dots in a colorful collage of football fans. But from our perspective, we were paupers at the king's palace—a stadium whose history and symmetry were steeped in nearly century-old tradition. Pilgrims who had driven nearly a thousand miles in a single (long) day to the gridiron mecca of Pasadena, California. Quacker backers wildly waving green-and-yellow pom-poms and blowing plastic duck lips in honor of our underdog heroes—a school whose unfamiliarity with these royal digs inspired shirts that said: "Just Like Clockwork— Every 37 Years, Oregon Goes to the Rose Bowl." Indeed, the last time the University of Oregon had appeared in the Rose Bowl, 1958, I was getting ready to enter kindergarten.

As the kickoff neared and the roar from the stands escalated, I remember momentarily thinking that this was a dream. Was this really Oregon lined up across the 35-yard-line? The school that had finished last in the Pac-10 conference the previous season and had lost two of its first three games this season? The school that, when I was sports editor of its newspaper 20 years before, had lost 14 straight games, including one 66-zip, and had drawn such small home crowds that people joked that it would be faster to introduce the fans to the players?

Now Oregon was playing in the most prestigious bowl game on the planet in front of a crowd ten times the size of those during the lean years. My sons looked awestruck at the surreal scene surrounding them. Millions of people watched from TVs in homes and bars and stores. Some 103,000 fans were on their feet, stomping and screaming, some of them waving roses in the blue Pasadena sky.

I have never felt so lonely in my life.

Because amid this magical mass revelry, I knew something that nobody else in the stadium knew; something that I had learned within hours of arriving in Los Angeles two days earlier; something that, coupled with the joy I was sharing with my sons, had me experiencing the highest high and the lowest low of fatherhood.

Paul, my brother-in-law's 16-year-old son, was dead.

• • •

Paul Scott Scandrett was born on October 24, 1978, the same day that my wife learned she was pregnant with my oldest son, Ryan. Because of that and other similarities, I've always thought Ryan and Paul enjoyed a link that went beyond their being cousins. To this day, it's hard for my wife's sister, Linda, and her husband, Greg, to see Ryan because he reminds them so much of the son they no longer have: independent, people-oriented, and down-to-earth. He had a penchant for mischief. A knack for a good one-liner. And a quiet faith in God.

He was the last of three children Linda and Greg would have. As our two families grew, we seldom lived close enough to spend much time together, so ours was one of those Christmas, Thanksgiving, and special occasions relationships.

I see Paul, his brother Brad, and my two boys belly flopping onto an old water-bed mattress in our backyard one summer.

I see him playing in a family baseball game—the day my youngest broke his first window with a line drive.

Mostly, I see him standing beside a Christmas tree, playing a shepherd boy in our family's traditional Christmas Eve play while one of his cousins (the innkeeper) holds up a sign saying, "No room." As director-by-default, I had, over the years, assigned Paul to be everything from the Ghost of Christmas Past to a store clerk, but more often than not, he played a simple shepherd boy. Though it was not a leading role, he always accepted it and, dish towel tied securely around his forehead, played it well.

A week before the Rose Bowl, my wife's side of the family—four generations, 22 people in all—gathered in Oregon for yet another Christmas Eve.

A week later, at 5:30 A.M., my sons and I left our Eugene, Oregon, home in a van with a friend and his two sons for Pasadena. Fourteen hours, three Big Mac stops, and a couple of potty breaks later, we arrived. After checking into the hotel, I weaved my way through the New Year's Eve celebrants in the lobby and phoned my wife to let her know we had arrived safely. I could barely hear above the lobby noise, but when she answered, it sounded as if she were sobbing.

My mind raced. "I have some terrible news," she said.

Grandma Klein, I thought. At 90, Sally's grandmother was wearing down; in fact, on Christmas Eve, she had surprised everyone by interrupting the present-giving to simply say how much she loved us all, as if she knew something we did not.

"It's Paul," Sally said.

Earlier in the day, he had been hiking with his 17-year-old brother Brad above the canyon-flanked Skokomish River southwest of Seattle. He had slipped and fallen some 40 feet into turbulent, icy water.

"They . . . think . . . he's . . . dead," she said. "They haven't found his body."

Paul? No, not Paul. No . . . no . . . no.

We talked some more. I stood in near disbelief. Should we come home? No, Sally said; the service wasn't to be held for five days. She had her sister—and best friend—Ann to lean on. Enjoy this once-in-a-lifetime experience, she said; even Greg, Paul's father, had said as much when he heard we were in Los Angeles.

Should I tell the boys and shatter the trip for them or wait until we returned? Neither one of us knew the right answer. I said good-bye, buried my face in my hands, and cried. As I wandered back to our hotel room amid people laughing, wearing New Year's Eve hats, and holding drinks, I was thinking: *This is not how the script is supposed to go.*

A street kid with a needle-pocked arm dies, but not the son of my brother-in-law, a small-town minister in Washington state.

An adult with a disease dies, but not my healthy nephew, the all-star soccer player, the kid who had just played an impish shepherd boy in the family Christmas play.

A 90-year-old grandmother in constant pain dies, but not a 16-year-old kid who, a week earlier, had spent the night with us. I had come home from work and heard strange noises coming from upstairs. "It's Paul and Ryan," said my wife. "They're having a burp-off."

Before returning to our hotel room, I decided to not tell the boys until we were home. The news would only taint the trip. There was nothing we could do. I would find a way to mask my pain. As I lay in the hotel room that night, everyone asleep but me, I remember dozing between dream and reality.

Paul is dead.

No.

Paul is dead.

No.

Paul is—

"Happy New Year!" yelled someone down the hall.

• • •

Death is ugly. Death is seeing your 44-year-old, unshaven brother-in-law for the first time after he has lost his son, almost too weak to stand, looking as if he has aged ten years in ten days.

Death is a house full of relatives and friends talking in library-soft voices.

Death is a table in the church lobby that's displaying childhood photographs and a model airplane and a soccer ball that no one will ever kick again.

Death is a vase of roses next to the portrait of a young man.

Even if your faith were as deep and wide as the love of God promised in all the Sunday school lessons, how could you deal with the death of your son? How could your lips even move, much less sing "Amazing Grace"? How could you ever walk to a pulpit again, much less proclaim the glory of God?

As I watched my brother-in-law and his family during the memorial service, I grieved for them and held tight to my wife and sons, having already tried on the thought of death to those nearest me.

A couple of months after Paul's death, Greg and I sat alone in his living room. Given my brother-in-law's grief, I had learned to accept long stretches of silence, because it often said what words could not. "I was at the computer, cleaning out programs," he said after a while, "when I came upon some stuff of Paul's. The computer asked me, 'Are you sure you want to delete?'"

He stopped, unable to talk.

"I wanted to scream—No!!! I don't want to delete. I didn't want it to be so . . . so final."

We drove to the spot where Paul had fallen, and we stood on a bridge, far above the frothy white water that pounded through a notch in the Olympic Mountains. Greg lamented that so many young people today regard life as cheap—not a privilege, but a pain. "What hurts is that Paul loved life," he said. "Why did it have to be someone who loved life so much?"

Why? Why? Why? A million whys, churning through our souls like the icy waters below.

Though we hadn't communicated much in the past, Greg and I began e-mailing each other—first only occasionally, then with growing consistency. As a pastor, he was forever under the congregational microscope; some members of his church felt that recovering from the death of one's son was like a military furlough: Once the period of time was up, say a month, you rejoin the regiment with a stoic sense of business-as-usual.

But it will never be back to business-as-usual for my brother-in-law or his family. Late at night, in the safety of cyberspace, Greg would bare his often-tormented soul with the click-click of computer keys.

He wrote of wanting someone to be held accountable for Paul's death. Why hadn't the Forest Service placed signs warning of the dangerous canyon slope? He wrote of trying to be strong for his wife and family when he felt no strength. He wrote of the listlessness of life. And of anger at God.

"I really miss Paul," said one e-mail message. "And the predominant emotion for me is anger. Anger at God. It is so intense sometimes that I fear I will not be able to preach."

• • •

He did. With the passage of time, Greg not only preached again, but did so with renewed fervor; with a certainty that had been steeled by a faith shaken but not shattered; with a faith strengthened by a willingness to finally say, "I do not understand. I may never understand. But, Father, I still believe."

Often when speaking, Greg would refer to the words of Isaiah 50:10: "Who among you fears the Lord and obeys the word of his servant? Let him who walks in the dark, who has no light, trust in the name of the Lord and rely on his God."

On Christmas Eve, nearly a year after Paul's death, our family theater group announced that the annual production would be presented by the Paul Scandrett Theater Company. Every play would be dedicated to the memory of the missing shepherd boy, reflecting the faith and fun that made him who he was.

The play was a comedy aimed at Paul's sister, Traci, and her new husband, Brandon. Greg laughed. Linda laughed. Everyone laughed. And I sensed healing, though I knew none of us—particularly Paul's family—would ever be the same.

A week later, I watched the 1996 Rose Bowl on TV. Seeing the stadium brought it all back: the best and worst day of my life exactly one year before. The day I was wrapped in a schizophrenic funk, one moment sharing the wonder of it all with my sons, the next minute wanting to shout to 103,000 people: "How can you all be so happy? Don't you understand? Paul is dead."

A Penn State fan, he would have been pleased with the outcome; the Nittany Lions won, 38-20. I told my sister-in-law I wish he had been there to see the game with us; he would have had a great seat. "He had a better one," she said.

Since that day, I think of Paul whenever I see a rose: petals of promise inextricably linked to the prickly thorns below. Joy and sorrow on the same life stem, waving in the blue Pasadena sky and, in a church lobby, dutifully guarding the sweet face that a father will never forget.

NEW EYES

I save things. I'm a compiler. A filer. My life is a museum that nobody ever comes to see (probably for good reason). I still have the cover of the first book I wrote, as an 11-year-old: *The H-Bomb Affair: A Man from U.N.C.L.E. Novel,* which had a first (and last) printing of one. The complete results of the 1970 Seaside (Oregon) Eight-Mile Beach Run, in which I only recently discovered that, in finishing eighty-second, I beat an ex-University of Oregon distance runner named Phillip Knight by 22 seconds. (Was it his humiliating loss to me that, two years later, inspired the man to develop faster footwear by launching a little shoe company called Nike?)

I've saved a photo of my VW Squareback's odometer at the precise moment, in 1975, that it hit 100,000 miles. Sand from the first time Sally and I walked on the beach together. A slip of paper that says, "As I am watching this (on TV), Neil Armstrong is walking on the moon." Seventeen years' worth of Father's Day cards. A bottle of Old Spice that belonged to my dad. And the golf ball (Pro Staff 2) I used when I broke 80 for the first time (a ball that is now the same color your teeth might me if you didn't brush them for 16 years, which is about how long it's been since I broke 80).

Am I pathetic or what? Why do I save all this stuff?

I suppose it is because I think it's important. Because I believe who we are now is linked to who we were then. Because, if we allow it, the past is like a benchmark that helps us see how much we've changed or how much we've stayed the same. Because, as happened to me the other night, we sometimes need to remember what it was like to be 17 so we can better relate to people in our family who are currently 17.

While rummaging through some old file cabinets—I have six of them, not counting boxes I use for the same purpose—I came across a manila folder labeled "Writing: Senior Year Of High School." An hour later, after coming back to the future, I had made three deductions: I wrote some pretty cheesy stuff, like a Christmas play in which an elf says to Mrs. Santa: "Take it easy, big momma, we're leaving." Second, I couldn't spell back then either. And finally, I had totally forgotten about the fear of growing up.

You see, I've been in something of a panic since September. That's when I went to the College Preparation Night at the high school where my son is a senior. After two hours of listening to people talk about SATs and ACTS and APs and FAFSAs; about the deadline for this and the deadline for that; and about the keen competition for scholarships, financial aid, and admission to schools, I came away feeling like a man trying to place his son on a moving train with limited seating.

I realized that some parents had been diligently following the Planning Your Future guides to the letter, and thus had opened college funds on their way home from the hospital after the delivery of their child, had helped their child decide a vocation by high school, and had made visits to campuses by the time the kid was a high school junior.

I, on the other hand, had siphoned off a considerable amount from the children's "education account" to such pursuits as taking the family on an 12-state vacation around the West (I rationalized that it was a *really* long field trip) and to the Rose Bowl (hey, two schools of *higher education* were playing each other, were they not?). Every visit to a campus that Ryan and I have made in the last few years has had something to do with us watching football or basketball games. And in terms of declaring a major—well, let's just say that while Ryan is a solid student, he pursues extracurricular activities with a bit more passion than academics.

Once he arrived home muttering about flunking a book review assignment. "My teacher said my book wasn't acceptable. She said we had to have read a *classic* and mine didn't qualify.

"I told her, 'Mrs. Fasold, how can you possibly say Jack Nicklaus's *Golf My Way* is not a *classic*?' "

Given this bombardment of college stuff, I did what any other self-respecting, asleep-at-the-spiritual-wheel father would do in a similar situation: I vowed that somehow my son would get on that train if I had to become the engineer myself.

First, I casually suggested—in the same way that the United States casually suggested that Iraq might want to consider loosening its grip on Kuwait—that Ryan retake his SATs to get higher scores. And I strongly suggested he take eight one-hour tutor sessions to help him get those higher scores.

I began littering his bedroom with literature on colleges I had requested. Pressuring him to start thinking about essays he might want to write. Peppering him with questions about what he wanted to do with his life. Asking him how his grades were looking.

By Christmas, I had built a file on colleges roughly the size of the Pentagon Papers. And continued to encourage Ryan with the same sensitivity that Bobby Knight uses on basketball refs:

Let's get that essay going, huh? Did you write to the golf coach at Whats-A-Matta U? Would you like to attend some classes at State U? How's that essay coming? What did you learn today at your SAT tutoring class? Can you get a recommendation from a counselor who knows you? OK, uh, can you get to know a counselor—preferably by Friday? And, say, how's that essay coming?

As the weeks passed, I tried to get a read on directions Ryan was leaning. Did he want to go to this college or that college? Or did he want to go to college at all? He wasn't sure what he wanted to do.

I had known what I wanted to be since fourth grade: a newspaper reporter. So even if it meant betraying my beloved Oregon State, it was a simple decision to go to the University of Oregon, which had a first-class school of journalism.

Why couldn't it be this simple for Ryan? Why was he making all this so difficult?

One night, sitting in my office, Ryan and I were talking about his essay. He didn't know how to begin it. I offered suggestions, but I wasn't connecting with him.

Why is he making this so hard? I thought. You just sit down and write it. That's what I did when I was in high school. That's what he should be able to do now.

I didn't say any of this to him; instead, I changed the subject. I said it must be exciting to be embarking on a whole new journey. Ryan muttered something in return, and when I asked him to re-mutter it, what he said was this: "It's kinda scary."

Given that, I did what any other shortsighted, me-first father would do: Instead of thinking about where that "kinda scary" came from—what equation led to that answer—I thought about all the time and effort I had put into getting all this college stuff organized. And his response? He's scared.

Scared? You want to know what scared is, kid? Scared is looking at those "What College Costs" charts that *Time* and *Newsweek* publish in their special college issues. Scared is having to fill out a FAFSA form, which is akin to a financial strip search. Scared is thinking that his mother and I won't have any money to retire on because we spent it all on him and his brother so they could go off and throw Frisbees for four years at about $100 a toss.

Of course, I didn't say any of that either. But I was peeved that while I was running after the train full bore,

Ryan was still back at the station, as if he didn't care about getting on. Which meant I had to pull harder on him. Which made me angry.

I mean, I had been young once. I wrote essays in my sleep. I hopped from high school to college as if I were simply walking from a store's deli section to the frozen foods case.

Scared? What is it with these nineties kids? I remembered my senior year as nine months of fun, the only perceived downers being a bad case of shin splints that ruined my cross-country season and a minor romance gone bad.

Then, when going through my file cabinet, I came across the "Writing: Senior Year of High School" file and made one of the most painful discoveries a father can make: that sometimes we're so worried about our sons pleasing *us* that we completely forget about *them*.

Sometimes we're so busy looking at life through 43-year-old eyes that we forget what it looks like through 17-year-old eyes. And if we do stick in the 17-year-old filter, it's often a filter whose lens has been so tainted by time that reality looks fuzzy. We see what we want to see, not what actually *is*.

Here's what I found in that "Writing: Senior Year of High School" file, the discovery that turned me from self-seeking father to humbled father: Life as a 17-year-old was kinda scary.

I wasn't nearly the happy-go-lucky student that I had remembered myself as. I didn't find a single essay that I had "sat down and whipped out." Instead, I found three gloomy short stories with some sentences that looked like Amtrak wrecks. The stories had one central theme: fear of the future.

Since September, I've been expecting Ryan to go from Relatively Carefree Kid to Adult with Precisely Planned Future in a few months. I've been thinking that the standard my son should be living up to is me, when in fact it's the One who created us both. And I've been forgetting that God might want something totally different from my son than I want from him.

After thinking about the three short stories and the realization they triggered, I left them on Ryan's bed, along with the following letter:

January 19, 1997

Ry:

Last night, while rummaging around for some stuff in my file cabinet in the shed, I came across some writing I did as a high school senior, the same age you are.

And I learned a few things:

First, I think I've been a bit harsh on you and your writing, comparing your 17-year-old mind to a 43-year-old mind. I'm sorry. Technically, you're every bit as good as I was when I was your age. Maybe better. All you need is experience and challenges. Just like in golf, you need to try some different courses, stretch yourself, be willing to fail. That's how you'll get better.

Second, since it's been 25 years since I was a senior in high school, I've forgotten some of those fears that come with that time period. The fear of life changing as you know it. The fear of having to "grow up." The fear of the unknown future.

In the last few months, I've been all wrapped up in the technical side of your going on to college—the applications, the money, the SATs, etc. What I've forgotten in all this is you and your feelings—many of them, I suppose, feelings of apprehension.

Some of my high school stories reflect that same apprehension. Though fiction, they reflect what was going on in my head at the time.

I'd forgotten what an unsettled year my senior year had been—dating a girl who didn't believe in the same God I did . . . trying to figure out what I wanted to do in the future . . . and realizing, as a very young Christian, that I lived in a world that went against the grain of my new beliefs, and had good, close friends whose beliefs were totally different than mine.

So if you get a chance, read this stuff, even if I'm not particularly proud of these stories. Some go nowhere, dropping off like roads to the Grand Canyon.

I pass them on to you only because I wrote them at the same age you are now—and thought you might find them interesting. In many ways, you are a more "together" kid than I was at that age. Your job. Your Sunday school teaching. Your ability to get along so well with both peers and adults. I'm not sure I was that secure as a high school senior. (I know I couldn't smooth a 5-iron like you can.)

Enough babbling. I end by simply saying I love you, I'm enjoying seeing you turn from a boy to a young man, and I am here for you if you want to talk. . . .

Love, Dad

I mentally save things. I'm a compiler of conscience. A filer of experiences. And when I filed away this lesson from winter, I couldn't do so without realizing one more reason why I had been so compulsive about getting on the college train.

As long as I concentrated on the logistics of getting my son into college—of dealing with SAT scores and GPAs and family financial contributions—as long as I concentrated on the gnarly process itself, I could neatly avoid the fear that lurked far back in my mind's filing cabinet.

The fear of saying good-bye to my son.

FINAL
SEASON

The other night, after the parents had all come to pick up their sons and I was picking up catchers' equipment, bats, and, of course, one forgotten mitt, it dawned on me that this was it: the last season I would coach one of my sons' baseball teams. Twelve seasons. Two sons. Hundreds of games. Maybe three decent umps. And thousands of memories, hidden in my mind like all those foul balls lost in the creek behind the Ascot Park backstop.

Sitting in the bleachers on this spring evening—everyone had gone—I found myself lost in thought. I found myself mentally walking along the creek, finding those long-forgotten foul balls and listening to the stories they had to tell.

The time our left fielder got locked in a Dairy Queen bathroom during a post-game celebration. The time I handed a protective cup to our new catcher and he thought it was an oxygen mask. The time a t-baller cleanly fielded a grounder, picked it up, and tossed it to his mom, who was sitting behind third base, reading Gone with the Wind.

For something that became more than a decade-long family affair, it had begun casually enough. While I was watching one of my five-year-old son's t-ball games in 1985, a manager asked if I would coach second base.

"Uh, *second* base?"

"Yeah. At this level, you need coaches at second base or the kids will forget to take a left and wind up at Safeway."

So I coached second base. And before long, our family's summers revolved around a diamond: me coaching, my wife, Sally, keeping score, and the boys playing. Like the Israelites trudging out of Egypt, we packed our equipment, lawn chairs, video camera, and 64-ounce drinks from diamond to diamond, week after week, summer after summer.

The time our right fielder turned up missing during a championship game, only to be found at the snack bar eating licorice and flirting with girls. The time we showed up at an empty field, only to discover I had read the schedule wrong and our game was actually ten miles away. The time we showed up on the wrong day for a tourney. (Do you see a pattern here?) The time I explained to my fifth-grade team that, because we had given up eighty-nine runs in the last four games, we needed to set a defensive goal.

"It's a six-inning game," I explained. "Let's just try to hold them to 12 runs per game. Two per inning. Can you do that?"

Silence. Then my philosophical right fielder spoke up.

"Coach," he said, "do we have to give up the runs even like that or could we, like, give up all 12 in the last inning?"

Our teams were more than a collection of kids. They were extended family, some of whom wound up sleeping overnight. And some of the boys desperately needed that. One year, of 15 players, only five had a mother and father living together under the same roof. Once, a boy missed practice because his uncle had been murdered. And sometimes I took kids home because nobody came to pick them up.

But I've always remembered the advice a coach at a clinic gave us: "Who knows? The six hours a week you spend with a kid might be the only six hours all week that he actually feels loved."

The out-of-control coach who pushed me off the field. The kid who didn't get picked for my team and sought revenge by firing a splat gun at our left fielder during a practice. Or the father who dropped off his son, Willie, and told him to get his own ride home; he and his girlfriend were going to a tavern to play darts. We went into three extra innings that afternoon, and the man's son played the game of his life, going all nine innings at catcher and, as dusk added drama to the scene, making the game-winning hit.

We tried to make it more than just baseball. With help from our sons, we established a team newspaper. A few times, I would put candy in a sack at second base and let players dig in every time they made an out. (Best defensive practice we ever had.) My wife Sally played DH—designated healer—with her ever-present cooler full of pop, and packages of frozen corn for the sprained ankles and bruised arms. Once, we had pizza delivered to the ball field just after we had lost to a team with one of those scream-and-yell coaches. I think we had more fun that night than the team that won.

In the years to come, we won games, we lost games, we lost baseballs—zillions of them. But for every ball we lost, we gained a memory. As a family, we laughed together, cried together, got dusty together, as if each of those hundreds of games was a microcosm of real life—which, I suppose, it was.

A weak-hitting kid named Cody stroking a three-run double and later telling his mom: "I try to stop smiling, but I just can't."

My oldest son becoming my assistant coach, and reaching a few kids in ways that I could not.

A rainy April evening, my entire team crammed into my parked Subaru station wagon as I stood outside under an umbrella, quizzing them on defensive situations.

Kids I coached as third-graders now taller than I was.

And, of course, the night we were going to win the city championship. Our team that year was a team of destiny. We won games we had no business winning. In the quarter finals, we needed three runs in the bottom of the last inning with the weakest part of the order at bat. We won. I could taste our first city championship ever.

But the game never got played. For the first time in two months, it rained. Instead of playing on a field of dreams with perfectly straight white lines and a public address system, some official handed me a bunch of medals and called us co-champs. I was crushed. Co-champs? There are no "co-champs" in baseball. There are winners and losers and nothing in between. Nobody ties in baseball.

Until now apparently. We had a sort-of-celebration at a pizza parlor. After everyone had left, the restaurant manager approached me, broom in hand. "Excuse me, but are you the coach of the Washington Braves?"

"I sure am," I said, suddenly feeling a flicker of pride. The guy was probably going to congratulate me on our wonderful season, I figured, and I prepared to shake his hand. Instead, he handed me the broom.

"Coach," he said, "your team trashed the indoor playroom. There's broken-up peppermint candy everywhere. Wanna help sweep?"

Somehow, that is not how I thought I would end this day of destiny: sweeping up broken candy in the playroom of a pizza parlor, all alone, on a rainy night.

Twelve seasons. Two sons. Hundreds of games. As a family, we had shared them all. What, I wondered, had we missed in the process? What had we given up in order to pursue what some might see as trivial?

Nothing. Because whether your family is together at baseball games or camping trips or rodeos or dog shows or soccer tournaments or swim meets, the common denominator is this: families together—a rarity in our busy times—

making memories. Learning lessons. Sowing seeds that can only be nourished by time.

Regrets? Only one. I wish Willie's father had considered his son more important than a game of darts, and had stayed to see him mobbed by teammates after making that game-winning hit. Everyone saw it but the people who needed to see it most.

5:22 A.M.

On the night after my father died, I stood in my old bedroom—a room that once was decorated wall-to-wall in *Sports Illustrated* photographs. It had become my father's catch-all room after I got married, and now was a reminder of who the man was. As a feature writer, I've learned that one way to understand profile subjects is to look at their surroundings. To see where they lived. To notice what they hung on the walls. And so, in preparing to write a eulogy for my father, I stood in what had been his surroundings.

Among the items I found on this August evening were two fishing poles, a paperweight that I had made for him in Cub Scouts, three camera lens filters, and the complete works, not of Shakespeare or Faulkner, but of Patrick McManus, the outdoor humor writer.

My father loved fishing and loved to laugh. For Christmas, you would give him a McManus book in the same way you would give a child a drum set—with great reluctance. Because he would spend the rest of the day reading his favorite passages aloud, without being asked to do so, and in some cases with being strongly encouraged *not* to do so. "Oh, listen to this part," he would say. "Oh, here's a great story." "Hey, check this out. . . ."

All but one of my father's jokes seemingly began, "These two guys were fishing" (the lone exception being a joke that began, "These two guys were *ice* fishing"). As I grew up, my father told the ice-fishing joke to anyone who would listen (and to some who would not):

> One guy is catching fish after fish. The other guy is getting skunked.
> "What's your secret?" the unsuccessful fisherman asks the successful one.
> "Moomahmoomeemormormsmorm."
> "Huh? I can't understand you."
> "Moomahmoomeemormormsmorm."
> "What? I still can't understand you."
> He spits something out of his mouth.
> "You have to keep your worms warm."

On one wall hung a quote from Izaak Walton, done in calligraphy by my sister:

> No life so happy and so pleasant as the life of a well-governed angler . . . we sit on cowslip banks and hear the birds sing, and process ourselves (by) these silent silver streams, which now glide so quietly by us. God never did make a more calm, quiet, innocent recreation than angling.

My father was the smell of dried salmon eggs, Prince Valiant pipe tobacco, and Old Spice, seemingly the cologne of an entire generation of men. He was squishy tennis shoes, much of his life, it seems, spent wading fly-fishing lakes or launching boats.

As I looked around, I notice on the walls not awards and degrees, but photographs. Not of him. Of other people. In many ways, my father was a loner. Not the guy in the group shot, but the guy behind the camera lens. Not a joiner or the life of the party, but someone you wanted there. For years, Mom had a cartoon on the refrigerator showing a lone man sitting on a blanket with a sandwich in his hand. Beneath it: "Warren Welch, self-employed, holds his annual picnic."

I found a 1949 college diploma from Oregon State, an advertisement for his *Trout in the High Country* movie and, on a drawing board, blueprints of his beloved 22-foot Catalina sailboat. As usual, he had been contemplating, shall we say, "modifications."

My father was the mad tinkerer. He was constantly improving cameras and boats, even if it meant adding two feet of length to a craft, which he did once. At season's start, no Welch boat has ever been launched with dry paint. At season's end, no Welch boat has been rolled onto a trailer without having undergone a number of changes. My father thought nothing of modifying parts of the boat, sometimes even while we were under sail.

On top of a desk, I found a photo of Dad and his closest friend in the world, his brother Bill. They fished together. Sailed together. Grew up together. Grew old together.

I found a Garfield T-shirt that said "Slow Jogger." A photo of his mother and father. Arrowheads he had found as a kid. A letter I wrote him on Father's Day 1990. And an item that said as much about my father as anything: a paintbrush stuck in hardened fiberglass.

My father's forte was not follow-through. He would sweep up the garage and leave the sawdust in piles. And he would routinely finish paint jobs and leave his brush in the paint (or, in this case, the fiberglass), which doesn't promote brush longevity. So my mom presented this to him as a little trophy to mockingly honor him for his ability to leave things undone.

But on that final weekend amid the towering pines of Central Oregon, my father followed through on something much more significant than a paintbrush or a garage floor: his life.

Mom and Dad rarely exchanged presents on anniversaries, but on this fiftieth anniversary, he surprised her with a gold bracelet. In a special dinner at the lodge, he praised my mother in front of the entire family, saying that marrying her was the smartest thing he had ever done. He proudly posed for pictures with his children and grandchildren. He hugged those of us who had to leave Sunday night.

For some reason, my son Ryan said later, Grandpa gave him an extra hug that evening. We parted and left for home.

The phone call jolted me just after 5 A.M. two days later. It was my sister, who had stayed on at the cabin with two of her children, my youngest son, Jason, and my folks.

"Bob, it's your sister," she said. "It's Daddy. The paramedics are here. He's having difficulty breathing."

In the previous 20 years my father had survived a hernia, cataract surgery, heart bypass surgery, prostate cancer, and me and five teenage friends of mine in a 900-square-foot beach cabin. My first thought was that I might have to miss a few days of work if they had to transport him to a hospital in Central Oregon. But as Linda went on, I realized this was different. I realized that 100 miles away, as I heard the paramedics scurrying around in the background, my father was dying.

"That's it," my sister said a few moments later. "Bob, I think he's gone. . . . He is. He's gone."

Just like that. Dead of congestive heart failure. Before this day, I had three time-of-days memorized as more significant than all others: 8:22 P.M. (pronounced man and wife), 10:53 P.M. (Ryan born), 2:35 A.M. (Jason born). Now: 5:22 A.M. (father died).

You go to sleep with your world in order, and you awaken to this. Suddenly, you're helping your mother and sister clean up a cabin that, only two days before, had been a place of celebration. Now it was a place of mourning. A light rain began falling, a wintry intruder on this summer stage.

When carrying some items out to my parents' car, I saw

my father's fishing creel and fly rod in the backseat and had to walk off in the woods and cry. It was as if I were nine years old again. It did not matter that I had never loved fishing as much as my father did, nor that our experiences together were three decades old. What mattered is that he would never use that fly rod again.

My father was not one for nursing homes; he had been diligent in helping my mother care for her father in one, but he said more than once that when his time came, he wanted to hike into one of his favorite lakes and never come out. I brought up that story as I drove my mother home over the Cascade Mountains that he loved so much, and back to the Willamette Valley where we lived. Noting that Dad had died at a nice resort in the mountains, I told my mother, "I guess he just took the deluxe plan."

My mother laughed. Then cried. That's how it is when you lose a man you've been married to for 50 years and one day.

You go to sleep with your world in order, and the next day you're talking to your mother about the man you both loved, but in past tense. You're driving by Suttle Lake, remembering the times you sat out there in the "Rotsa Ruck" boat on cool summer mornings, fishing. And the time he allowed you to tie up the boat one evening and, after an overnight windstorm, the boat was found a mile away the next morning, beached at an outlet stream, and how he wasn't even mad. And you think of all the little lakes hidden among the hundreds of miles of Douglas firs that he had hiked to, often by himself.

You listen to your mother, who's trying to process what this means. A woman who has loved this man since she met him as a high school junior in 1942. Who waited through a war for him to come home. Who clung to him in sickness and in health, through job losses and car accidents and bypass surgeries and illnesses and the deaths of parents—not because marriage was incessant bliss, but because the two of them had made a commitment, and they came from a generation that, though not without fault, has honored its commitments better than my own.

You go to sleep with your world in order, and suddenly you're at a funeral home and they're asking you what kind of urn you want your father's ashes in. They hand your mother an envelope that contains his wallet and wedding ring. And ask if she would like an American flag presented to her at the service, on behalf of the U.S. Navy.

Once back home, I see the newspaper advertisement that was published in the local paper two days before—on my parents' anniversary. It is an ad for the photography studio that had taken my parents' fiftieth wedding anniversary photo, and beneath a smiling picture of the two of them says: "Today's portraits can't be made tomorrow."

Two days later, we gather at a church for the memorial service. A minister reads my mother's description of how they met, the story of how her parents forbade her from dating a college man, and how she argued that he wasn't technically a college man because he wouldn't be registering until the day after their date.

My sister offers a beautiful reflection. I read my eulogy, complete with visual aids, including the paintbrush stuck in the hardened fiberglass.

A trio sings a favorite song of my parents: the Christy Minstrel's "Today."

> Today while the blossoms still cling to the vine
> I'll taste your strawberries, I'll drink your sweet wine
> A million tomorrows shall pass away
> Ere I forget all the joy that is mine, today.

Until now, I have kept my composure well—much better than expected. But as this song begins, I weep, as do my mother and sister. My wife, amazingly selfless through this whole ordeal, gently takes my hand and puts it on top of my mother's.

I cry for all the memories. For the 14-year-old boy in the photograph proudly holding that trout at Sparks Lake. For the young sailor who went off to war. For the young father playing knee football with his son. For the middle-aged man whose *Trout in the High Country* dreams never came true. For the aging father who nevertheless signed his letters with bold Xs and Os. For the man whose last words to me were, like him, more practical than poetic, but embodied the essence of love: "Drive carefully, Bob."

I cry for all the joy that is mine today.

FAR SIDE
OF THE BARN

W hile researching the Mennonites of Oregon's
Willamette Valley for a newspaper story, I spent
an afternoon with a man who ran a painting
business with his teenage son. On this particular summer day,
the two were painting a barn roof. The father tethered his son
to a rope and stood on the ground, holding one end of the
rope. The son climbed a ladder to the barn roof, carefully
made his way up the near side, then disappeared down the far
side to roll on the paint as if mopping a floor.

When he was younger and worked alone, the man would
paint a roof by himself. He would rig a system of tethers that
would allow him the freedom to move and yet prevent him
from falling. When his son began painting, the man at first
placed the boy on short tethers. And as the young man grew
older and proved himself trustworthy, the father gave him
more rope.

Soon it would be time for the son to paint alone. Time for
the father to stand back and watch as the young man
climbed the ladder, looked back, and disappeared over the
peak of the barn's roof.

As the winter of separation arrives, I am that father. My oldest son is about to disappear over the peak of the barn's roof.

It is the most fascinating and frightening experience I've ever had as a father. Fascinating, because as my son prepares to graduate from high school and leave our home, I see signs that the same boy once afraid to even climb a ladder is now high on the roof, with ropes firmly anchored in the right place. Frightening, because for the first time not only do I realize that I can't hang on to him anymore, but I realize something else: I'm losing more than a son. I'm losing a friend.

As a high school senior, he now has one foot firmly planted on each side of the roof's peak. When one of his high school's most popular English teachers abruptly retired, it was my son, I learned, who created an ad in the student newspaper to thank the man for all he had given to the school's students. That, I thought to myself, was a mature thing to do. He's becoming a man who honors others and, in so doing, honors God.

The other night, even though he had an important golf tournament the next morning, he helped pick up driving-range balls so a teammate of his wouldn't have to work so late. What more could an earthly father or heavenly Father want? Isn't that vintage Philippians 2:3, considering others' needs more important than our own?

Recently, we were walking on the beach, discussing the novels he had read during his high school years. "They're all about problems, but offer no solutions," he said. *Profound*, I thought. *He's showing wisdom in realizing man's futility without God.*

But when I was driving down the street the other day in the pickup I had loaned him for a few days, I felt something sticky on my hand and realized that he had left three "used" Tootsie Roll Pop sticks in the console between the bucket seats. And I reached in my golf bag the other day only to find one of my last remaining balls had a half-inch hole drilled through it (Ryan was using my golf balls again to make gearshift knobs for his car).

Responsible? Mature? He's still just a kid.

But if he's got one foot in manhood and the other in boyhood, I suppose I'm doing some straddling of my own.

Part of me wants him to grow up, leave home, experience new places, meet new people, and test his faith in an often-faithless world. And part of me wants him to stay age 5 or 12 or 17 forever, asking me, as he once did, how God can hear everyone's prayers at the same time and playing catch with me out back and sitting around the kitchen table on rainy nights, talking about everything from death to Oregon Duck football.

Part of me wants him to learn all the lessons that can only be learned through risk and vulnerability. And part of me wants to protect him from a world that can be cold and cruel.

Part of me wants him to learn to live without me. And part of me dreads the inevitability that he will.

This is winter—the season of separation. The season of Christmas-card scenery and wind-chill deaths, nature as beauty and the beast. And so it is with relationships, winter being a Jekyll-and-Hyde blend of bonding together and breaking apart.

To some degree, however, fathers and sons experience separation their entire lives. At the turn of the century, my grandfather experienced separation at age seven when the courts ruled that his father couldn't see him or his mother anymore because my great-grandfather was abusive.

My grandfather grew up and became a father and watched his son—my dad—sail off to war.

My dad survived that war, became a father, and watched me choose some life paths that weren't his own; ours was a values separation that, though not bitter, put distance between us.

I grew up, became a dad, and have realized countless points of separations: the first time we left Ryan in the church nursery. The first day of kindergarten. The first time he stayed overnight with a friend and our house seemed so lonely.

My journal recalls the day Ryan went in for hernia surgery at age eight:

> Just before the operation, you and I were alone, waiting. You looked so small. So young. So innocent. You threw your arms around me and told me you were scared, which made me want to cry, partly because, as an eight-year-old, you don't throw your arms around me as much as you used to. And much as I wished you could have avoided this experience, I needed that hug. When it was time to go, you walked off with the nurse. Just before you went into the operating room, you glanced back, then grabbed the nurse's hand and held it tight.
>
> It was hard giving you up, even if it was for something as relatively simple as a hernia operation. It's times like that—waiting for the surgeon to return with news of the operation—that a father realizes how much he loves his son.

The first time we left him for an extended vacation. The day we had to enroll Ryan in the fourth-grade class of Miss Sofie, a drill-sergeant teacher who we feared would eat our son alive; in fact, we had talked to the principal about placing him in another class. No dice. When we walked him to the class, we did not want to let him go; I felt like Abraham taking Isaac to the sacrificial altar.

Other separations followed: the day he first drove off in a car. The weekend at the beach cabin when, for the first time, he announced he was bored and wished he had someone other than us around. The job at the golf course that meant missing family dinners.

Soon, he will be missing more than family dinners. He will be off to college. On his own.

Separation. Once, it was leaving him at kindergarten, now it's financial-aid applications. Letters from colleges and the Air Force, the Marines, the Coast Guard, all of them saying the same thing, at least in my mind: Leave your parents, kiddo. Get a life. A new life.

But, I remind myself: Like the Mennonite father, our job as fathers is to work our way out of a job. Remember what your friend Pastor Rick Taylor told you: From the moment our children are born, they are in a slow process of pulling away from us, learning to live without us.

Those last five words stab like a dagger; we all want to be wanted, needed. But I know Rick is right. God has granted me temporary custody of two sons; my job as a father is to do everything I can to prepare them to live on their own—independent of me, dependent on God.

And part of that is teaching them that as they disappear over that barn roof, the rope that will hold them most securely—eternally secure—is not made of fiber and held by their father, but made of faith and held by *the* Father.

FATHERS, SONS, AND WAR: PART I

I n the cultural swirl of the sixties, Timothy Ownbey and Larry Browning met as teenagers in Springfield, Oregon, a blue-collar community that was far less likely to be protesting the Vietnam War than sending its boys to fight it.

They had lots in common: roots in North Carolina, where their families had lived only 20 miles apart before both moved to Washington state and then to Oregon. Birthdays within two months of each other. Fathers who not only were the same age, but who had the same first name, Jay, and were both ex-Navy men who had fought in the South Pacific in World War II. Fathers who, amid a generation gap that gouged many such relationships, remained tight with their sons.

Tim and Larry grew up in different churches, but went to the same school and enjoyed the same activities—everything from waterskiing to cruising Willamette Street in the city next door: Eugene.

In some ways, they were different. Tim drove a red 1957 Chevy, Larry a 1968 Roadrunner. Tim was a prankster—the

Dennis the Menace of Thurston High, the kid who once un-
leashed crickets during one of Pastor Barnes's sermons at
Bethel Assembly of God Church. Larry was Tim's straight
man—the guy who set up Tim for the great one-liners. Tim
was something of a Pied Piper, a guy who people—even
adults—just liked to be around. Larry happily followed.

By the time the two graduated from high school in the
late sixties, these strands of similarities and differences had
woven themselves into a tight friendship that seemed destined to last a lifetime.

But it wasn't to be.

The other day, as a winter wind whipped an American
flag, I stood in Springfield Memorial Cemetery, having
stopped to see two headstones about 500 feet apart, and was
reminded that the story of Timothy Ownbey and Larry
Browning is about much more than friendship.

It's about faith.

It's about home.

It's about fathers watching their sons go off to war.

• • •

In 1969, when Tim Ownbey was sitting in the recruiter's
office, one of the questions on the form blindsided him:
"When is the best time to notify next of kin in case of death
or injury?"

"I'm not planning on getting killed," Tim told the officer.

"Well, son," said the sergeant, "you're not going to a
party."

Tim paused, then signed on the dotted line. His thinking,
like Larry's, was that college—and a deferment from the
draft—wasn't a realistic option. Better to enlist than to be
drafted, they figured. And so the two did, becoming part of
the 80 percent of U.S. soldiers in Vietnam who hailed from
working-class and poor backgrounds.

In January of 1969, when Oregon was buried beneath a
rare record snowfall, Tim's mother had worried when

"Timmer" was doing belly flops off the roof into the three feet of powder below. A year later, as she prayed with her son on the morning he would leave for Vietnam, that worry seemed trivial.

Mabel hugged him good-bye, peeked out the window, and watched him turn and look back at the house one last time. In the early morning darkness, Jay and Tim drove to the Eugene Airport. Little was said.

Oftentimes, father-son closeness isn't measured as much in words exchanged as in experiences shared. And as Jay watched the jet grow small in the southern sky, en route to San Francisco, he thought of hunting and fishing with his son; of Tim working for him in the family construction business; and of the two of them playing on the same church-league softball teams over the years. In the last game, with three innings to go, the team manager wanted to take Tim out of the game.

"Leave him in," said Jay, almost surprised at his boldness. "Where he's going, he won't have much chance to play baseball."

Even after the plane had disappeared into the clouds, even as, behind him, people hustled and bustled to and from their flights, the father just stood there and watched the empty sky.

Six months later, Larry Browning and his father, Jay, arrived at the same airport for the same reason. Though it wasn't perfect, they had built a solid relationship in the last 19 years. In many ways, Jay was an older version of Tim: a guy that people—even kids—just liked to be around.

A log-truck driver, Jay Browning would arrive home Friday afternoon after a week-long job, driving his self-loading rig, and the neighborhood kids would clamor around him as he passed out his always-handy candy. He would wake up Larry and his older sister each morning with a Navy whistle that they detested but learned to live with.

While Larry nurtured a quiet Christian faith, his father proudly wore his on his sleeves. Taking Larry to a car race, he would say, "I'll meet you in the stands in 15 minutes," then swoop through the parking lot, placing Bible tracts on cars.

Though no Browning had ever been a pastor, Jay Browning was the next-best-thing to one. Church was his second home; he loved nothing better than a pastor who could preach a soul-wrenching sermon. Once, father and son went to a revival meeting. Jay loved it, and offered continuous "Amens!" Larry was petrified. Afterward, when he told his father he wouldn't be going to another service like that, Jay just laughed.

Jay was like that. He didn't punish those who expressed their faith more subtly than he did. And he wouldn't allow legalism to eclipse compassion. When Larry made the junior varsity basketball team despite being the shortest kid to try out, he discovered that practices would be on, among other nights, Wednesdays: youth night at church.

His mother said, sorry, he must go to church. His father overruled her. "Let the kid play ball," he said. "He earned it."

When Larry slipped into the post-high-school party scene, his father didn't approve, but neither did he condemn his son. He just kept loving him, even if it wasn't easy for him to say.

At 18, Larry felt God tugging at his heart. Though he had made a commitment to Christ as a youth, he felt a need to recommit. He had gone to a youth revival and felt the Spirit stirring inside. Afterward, he went to the pastor to find out what the stirrings meant.

"Call me Monday," said the pastor, "and make an appointment."

Larry never called. He had walked up to that pastor thinking he had made a life-changing decision—a decision to follow the God of the universe. But the pastor's nonchalant response stung, and Larry thought to himself: *Maybe my decision wasn't so important after all.*

The memories swirled as the two waited for the plane to

load. When Larry's flight was called, father and son hugged. They cried. "I love you, son," Jay told Larry. For the first time, Larry faced the reality that he might never again see this man. And for some reason, as the jet winged its way out of Oregon to California, what concerned him most was one unanswered question: Was his father proud of him?

• • •

Tim Ownbey arrived in Vietnam on January 31, 1970. His contract with the Army: one year, then home for six months of stateside service and a discharge. He was a gunner on an armored personnel carrier—a tank-like vehicle armed with a .50-caliber machine gun. He was part of the Black Horse armored 11th Cavalry Regiment that fought around Quan Loi, near the Cambodian border, 25 miles north of Saigon.

The ways of war came hard and fast. Five weeks into his stint, Tim was shot in the shoulder by Viet Cong gunfire in a battle in which eight American soldiers would die, 18 would be wounded, and Tim would earn the Bronze Star for his attempt to rescue a downed pilot.

"Bam, my left arm was already bleeding and my face and hair," he wrote in a letter home. "But I couldn't feel it. I tried to shoot with one arm, (but) my arm muscle just slowly dropped and I couldn't use it."

He slid off the armored personnel carrier and passed out. Fellow soldiers dragged him to a chopper. The carrier exploded after an enemy blast.

He recuperated at a hospital on the South China Sea, then returned to action. He wrote home diligently. He told his parents of snakes and leeches, scorching heat during the day and pounding rain at night, all-night watches and an unseen enemy.

He sent home photographs: groups of young men in khaki fatigues and no shirts who looked like a junior varsity basketball team celebrating a victory. Corny smiles and flexed muscles. Bronze, skinny upper bodies that had more filling out to do. The odd juxtaposition of innocence and M-16s.

He wrote about his fellow soldiers, like Frank, the first black man he had ever known. "He's like my brother," Tim wrote, "cause there ain't nothing he won't do for me."

Of his faith in God. "Don't worry about me. I'll take care of myself, with a little help from Him. Whatever has happened, and will happen, is in His plan, so it's all OK."

And of the cold realities of war:

> We were on a dismount and the point man must have just missed a personnel mine, but the second didn't and he lost both legs from the knees down and the men in front and rear of him were hurt but not bad. The radio man in charge yelled how bad is he and I yelled back so the wounded guy wouldn't hear me and said, "Bad" and Lester, the hurt guy, said, "Hey, Tim, tell 'em my legs are blowed off" and smiled and gave me the peace sign and I wanted to cry then.

Mostly, Tim wrote about something he longed for more than anything else: home. In one letter, he drew a picture of his hand, an X on the palm representing God, the center of his life, and X's on the fingers representing family, his girlfriend, his boat, and his dream car, a Chevy Camaro: "I know I have more waiting for me back in the world than anybody."

He sent money home so he and his dad could go in together and buy a ski boat—a used 14-foot Glaspar.

"Dad," he wrote in one letter, "I always felt kinda proud when you would say, 'I've never seen anybody who could stay calmer and not get excited when deer hunting than Tim.' Well, you should be proud because you and Ray B. taught me all. Now I do get excited. A lot in fact. But it's not for meat or sports. It's for my life."

• • •

In June, a commercial jet touched down on a landing strip in Bien Hoa, about 100 miles from where Tim was fighting. Among the fresh troops who stepped off the plane into the sultry Vietnam air was another kid from Springfield, Oregon: Tim's friend, Larry Browning.

Larry, an infantryman in the First Battalion, 12th Cavalry, Delta Company, was assigned to a unit that was fighting on the Cambodian border about 100 miles north of where Tim was. Like Tim, Larry learned the horrors of war about a month after he arrived.

On that morning, he met a soldier from the Midwest who, over a cup of hot chocolate, told Larry that he had been married in September and his wife was expecting a baby soon—a son, the doctor said. Half an hour later, that soldier was dead, along with three others, after a Vietcong ambush that also wounded eight.

That night, the 34 soldiers left from the 45-man unit made a perimeter around the bodies, awaiting morning and helicopters to evacuate their fallen comrades. And Larry Browning learned the hell known as war. It had nothing to do with the glorified versions he had seen on TV, and it had everything to do with separation: from family, from friends, from life on earth. It had less to do with feeling pain than feeling nothing.

More numbness would follow. After spending two weeks in a delta area with almost no dry land, Larry developed faliculitis, a serious infection that caused his feet to swell up so badly he could hardly lace his boots. Then he came down with malaria. Like Tim, he spent time in a hospital on the coast. After that, he was reassigned to an engineer compound where he became an air-traffic controller for the 11th Aviation Pathfinder Team.

July became August and August September. Larry learned that he would be eligible for two weeks of R & R, meaning he could be home for Christmas.

Meanwhile, down south, Tim continued his letters home. He accepted his father's offer to join him in the construction business when he got home. The chances looked good for him being home for good by Christmas, he wrote.

"I'm OK and happy and doing fine, but getting sicker for home as my time gets shorter," he wrote on September 27. "Four months, then freedom." Beside it, he drew a childlike picture of an airplane with an arrow pointing from South Vietnam to the United States.

At home, Tim's father, Jay, had a premonition that shook him deeply. He sensed Tim in so much danger and felt so helpless that he pictured himself actually going to Vietnam, grabbing his son, and telling anyone who tried to stop him: "This is my son, and he's coming home with his family where he belongs."

Instead, in mid-October, Jay sent a letter to Tim, encouraging him to remember the times they had hunted together. About keeping extra quiet. About being extra careful.

The letter was returned unopened, shortly after his son's body arrived home. Timothy Ownbey was killed October 25, 1970, when a land mine exploded. He was 20 years old.

His father looked at the letter, crumpled it, and threw it in the fireplace. If only he had sent it sooner, he said to himself, his son might still be alive. If only . . .

Back in Vietnam, Larry Browning was scanning a copy of the *Army Times* in early November, when he came upon the killed-in-action list. When he saw the name, he couldn't believe it. *Must be a mistake*, he thought. *Not Timmer*. But as he read further—" . . . from Springfield, Ore . . ."—he realized it was Tim. The Pied Piper was dead.

Larry had missed the memorial service. Missed Pastor Barnes eulogizing the young man who had once brought crickets to church. Missed it all. Instead, he was sitting in a war-torn country 15,000 miles from home. By now, God had become almost a distant memory to Larry and, thus, was little comfort. Nor did he find much comfort in letters from home, one of which said his parents were praying fervently that he would be home for Christmas on his R & R. All Larry knew was one of his closest friends in the world was dead.

The orders didn't come through for Larry's R & R at Christmas. On December 24, he was away from his base camp, on a helicopter flight to some units in the field, when it happened. The chopper landed at a U.S. camp. Someone asked if Larry would mind monitoring the radio for a little while. Sure, he said.

A few minutes later, one of the scratchy messages surprised him.

"Repeat," he said.

"Is Browning there?"

"Yes," said Larry. "This is Browning."

"You need to catch the first flight back to base."

"Why?"

"We'll tell you when you arrive. Just get here. And, by the way, do you have dress greens?"

On the flight to the base, Larry considered the possibilities. Surprise R & R? Home for Christmas after all! But what about the dress greens? Why wouldn't they tell him anything? What could it be?

When he arrived at the base five hours later, his captain welcomed Larry into his office. His face was ashen. Something was wrong.

"I don't know how to tell you this, son," he said, his eyes growing moist. "It's your father. He's been killed."

Second Spring

A time of beginning anew

Summer and winter, and spring-time and harvest,
Sun, moon and stars in their courses above,
Join with all nature in manifold witness
*To thy great faithfuness, mercy and love.**

In the father-son theater, First Spring sets the stage for all that will follow: hope, dreams, growth, change, conflict and, perhaps, resolution. But there is no final act, because this relationship is ongoing.

Roles change. A son becomes a father. A father becomes a grandfather. A prodigal son comes home; a wayward father returns. At times, a son even switches roles with his father, and winds up taking care of the man who once took care of him. The only constant in this Second Spring is a bond that abides between two men.

As with the essence of Easter, not even death brings the curtain to a close. Because fathers who lose a son are inextricably linked to that son, and will forever be influenced by the life—and death—of that boy. Likewise, sons who lose a father learn to play a new part, but the spirit of the man lives on each time they take the stage.

Second Spring, like fall, is a time of change. For many, it is a time of stepping out of the spotlight and playing a supporting role: adviser, consultant, friend. A time of reconciliation.

Above all, it is a time of beginning anew.

* From *Great Is Thy Faithfulness*, by Thomas O. Chisholm © 1923. Renewal 1951 Hope Publishing Co.

FATHERS, SONS, AND WAR: PART II

I t is late spring 1997. A silver-haired man and a middle-aged man greet each other with a gentle hug at Springfield Memorial Cemetery. Two men bound not by blood, but by broken hearts. Kindred spirits linked by long-ago losses. Hometown neighbors knit by a sad symmetry: a 44-year-old father who lost a 20-year-old son, and a 20-year-old son who, two months later, lost a 44-year-old father.

Jay Ownbey and Larry Browning come to this place occasionally to remember two men who died 15,000 miles apart—one in Vietnam, the other in the nearby foothills—and are now buried within a few hundred feet of each other.

"I suppose we both feel a little like we were robbed," says Larry.

Larry Browning's father, Jay, died in a log-truck accident three days before Christmas of 1970. He had gotten up that morning and had a premonition of danger. The Oregon winter was tightening its grip; the ice and snow that usually stayed high in the Cascades had slunk into the foothills, where Jay Browning and his crew were hauling timber. That

made logging—already one of the most dangerous occupa-
tions in the country—all the more dangerous. But Jay figured he would bring home one more load before Christmas.

He never made it home. Rolling down a steep, twisting
road later that afternoon, he lost control of his fully loaded
truck and was either thrown from the cab or jumped, dying
shortly thereafter.

Larry remembers no Christmas in 1970. Instead, he remembers questions, and one in particular: "Why, God?"
Sometimes the present is too close to see, and so it wasn't
until years later that Larry wondered if his father had died to
save his son. Because of his father, Larry had been set free
from the death zone of Vietnam.

Twenty-seven years later, Larry realizes that his father
has been dead longer than Larry knew him alive.

Meanwhile, Jay Ownbey will occasionally imagine how
old his son would be if he were still alive. It's easy. He would
be the same age as Larry, who turned 47 in 1997.

What has time begot? Pain, to be sure; for these two men,
not a day passes without a thought of what could have been.
Jay still hunts deer, but it's never been the same without Tim.
And Bing Crosby's "I'll Be home for Christmas" will forever
be a reminder to Larry of how, with a day's difference in
Vietnam-to-United-States time, he did get home for
Christmas that year—only for his father's funeral.

Yet in the darkness, a light flickers. Besides the loss itself,
death stings in another way for fathers: the fear that the
world will forget about their sons. It's a scary thought, that a
life that meant so much to them could be forgotten by others,
blown away by the winds of time.

In fact, years after his son's death, Jay had seen a classmate of his son wearing an American flag upside down, and
the rage rushed through him with volcanic force. Whether
the war was just or not, his son had died for that flag, and nobody was going to disgrace it by wearing it on a jean jacket
upside down. He lunged at the young man before others
pulled him back.

But in August 1996, something happened to remind Jay Ownbey that his son had not been forgotten. The replica Vietnam War Memorial came to nearby Eugene, and for four days the public turned out to look at the names of some of the 59,475 soldiers who had died in that war. When the weekend viewing was over, a woman who had volunteered to lead people to specific names was oddly touched by one name—a name that was requested far more than any other name on the wall: the name of Timothy Ownbey.

"I don't know who he was," said the woman, "but he must have been pretty special."

Indeed he was. Because he was more than just a name on the wall. He was a community's friend. A mother's hope. A father's son. When the (Eugene) *Register-Guard* newspaper ran a Sunday feature piece about Timothy Ownbey, the phone started ringing at Jay and Mabel Ownbey's house. Complete strangers called to comfort them, to offer prayers, to thank them for their sacrifice. People sent letters and cards, 26 years after Tim had died.

A relatively new neighbor next door brought over a meal, hugged Mabel, said she had had no idea what they had been through.

Down the street, on Veteran's Day, a man who hardly knew the Ownbeys but had read the article placed a large American flag and a small American flag in front of his house. Why two? asked a neighbor. One, the man said, was to honor all the men and women who had given their lives in combat for our country.

"The other," he said, "is for Timothy Ownbey."

If Jay Ownbey worried about his son being forgotten, Larry Browning wondered what his father would think of him today. As a young man, he had battled the demon of drugs in the post-Vietnam, post-father years. He had none of his father's boldness when it came to dealing with people; in fact, once, in a community college speech class, he walked to the podium and froze with fear. He had lost his childlike faith, his trust in God buffeted by a pastor who seemingly didn't care, and by war and death.

Were his father alive today, Larry sometimes wondered, would he be proud of who his son had become? The question still gnawed at him as it did the morning he last saw his father alive at the Eugene Airport.

Yes, Larry has ultimately decided, his father probably would be proud. Because now, if Mr. Browning were alive and were to show up at one particular evangelical church in Oregon and listen to one particular pastor, he would be reminded of this: Sometimes the seeds of faith planted by fathers in their sons take time to germinate. And sometimes they bear minimal fruit. But on occasion the seeds that have survived the coldest winters sprout most gloriously come spring.

Mr. Browning would know that because the man preaching the sermon in that particular church would be his son: Pastor Larry Browning.

CEILING
STARS

It is spring, and I am not the father I used to be. I was reminded of that last night when we invited a young couple from our church over for dinner. They brought along their two-year-old son and six-month-old daughter. While we ate, the mother told the story of how, earlier in the day, the little boy had taken a couple of dinner forks and stuck them in the "Insert Tape" portion of their VCR.

I found that a particularly hilarious story and so, naturally, pressed "Rewind" on my mind's VCR, to see if I could pull up a similar memory with my own two sons, now 17 and 14. What I discovered, instead, was a small red light flashing in that deep, dark abyss of my brain that said: "No Tape."

VCRs, you see, had not been invented yet when my sons were the ages of our guests' kids. So I had no tape of this experience. This realization, of course, made me feel very old and stuffy, as does seeing young couples with 18-wheel, leather-seated baby strollers that have better shocks than most cars I've owned. So does going to the annual Coburg

Antique Fair every September and seeing Star Wars action figures on table after table. R2-D2 as an antique? Impossible.

But I digress. The point is that all this change reminds me I am not the father I used to be. I was a father in a spring long ago. Now I am father in a Second Spring.

I used to be a father who played knee football with my sons, cross-country skied with one of them in a backpack, and prayed with them at "nigh-nigh" time.

Sometimes we would turn off the lights and lie on our backs, staring at the green fluorescent stars stuck on the bedroom ceiling, and pretend we were camping out. And as we lay there, I would announce it was time to play "Ask Anything"—my nightly way of encouraging them to ask deep, theological questions that had been haunting their toddler minds. And they would ask deep theological questions like: "Do police officers have homes?" and "Do the Seahawks football players get to keep their uniforms if they quit the team?"

Now I am a father who fills out FAFSA (Free Application for Federal Student Aid) forms, which, near as I can tell, are designed to make me look like a millionaire so nobody will have to give my kid any financial aid for college. *(Line 216: Amount of money that's slipped beneath the cushions of your living-room sofa . . .)*

I am a father who loans golf clubs to his son, pays for rebuilt transmissions, and explains the theme of hypocrisy in *The Scarlet Letter.*

I am a father who drives my youngest son places. Minutes ago, I received a phone call from Jason, asking if I might bring him home from Justin's house, where he and his friend have been, as they say, "jamming." I did so. Not only that, but I was given the distinct privilege of carrying his amplifier up the stairs to his bedroom, where I was informed that, although he has owned his bass guitar only two days, he already knows how to play the theme song from *Chariots of Fire.*

This, of course, got me thinking about how I've wanted for years to show that movie to the boys because it has such an honorable message about those values that our culture has discarded these days: courage, commitment, and faith. My oldest saw it, but probably doesn't remember the honorable message, since he was two years old at the time.

It seems like *Chariots of Fire* came out about seven or eight years ago. It actually came out 16 years ago, in 1981. But time flies when you're raising children.

In the film credits of life, one minute you are Superman, the next, Third Tall Man.

Last week, Ryan showed surprising concern when informed that, because of a golf commitment of my own, I would be out of town the weekend before his state golf tournament. Touching, I thought; he probably wanted some last-minute pointers from the old man. Or one of my patented pep talks.

"But I'll be back for your tournament," I said.

"Good," he said, obviously relieved. "I wanna use your wedge."

I am not needed as much as I once was. That isn't a regret, just a reality. Ten years ago I was my sons' ticket to nearly everything; now, they get around without me. Ten years ago, I had the answer to everything; now, my 14-year-old's math is too complicated for me to help. Ten years ago, I taught my oldest son to play golf; today, he teaches me.

While playing H-O-R-S-E with my sons, I used to purposely miss shots or take impossible-to-make shots—"left-handed hook while hanging from the downspout"—to make the game tight. Last Saturday, I got an "H-O" on one of the boys and heard—at least in my mind—ABC's Al Michaels shout, "Do you believe in miracles?" as he had after the U.S. Olympic ice hockey team stunned Russia in 1980.

According to grainy old 8mm films that our family shows every millennium, I used to take Jason and pretend he was a basketball, slowing threading him through a five-foot-high hoop. I used to go across the street from our house in snowy Central Oregon and slide down custom-made inner-tube runs with my pint-sized sons on my chest. I used to run on the beach with my sons, pretending we were in that

opening scene from *Chariots*, the young men striding grace-
fully along the seashore in slow motion, which is not all that
easy to re-create in real life. I used to play backyard football
and tell my sons-the-quarterbacks to throw the ball as far as
they could; I could run down anything they threw.

Now, they worry about overthrowing me, not under-
throwing me. Now I'm the guy who moves the car out when my
youngest wants to shoot hoops. I get foul balls out of gutters. I
say things like, "When I was a kid . . ." and the boys roll their
eyes and say, "You're always saying that: When I was a kid . . ."

We still pray together, though not every night. We don't
look up at the fake sky at night because the fluorescent stars
on the ceiling have all fallen from the sky, thanks to a celes-
tial paint job a few years back. And we don't play nightly
versions of "Ask Anything" anymore. It's a more spontaneous game these days, and not nearly as easy as it used to
be for the Answer Man.

> "Why would a loving God allow (Cousin) Paul to die?"
> "Why shouldn't I quit my job?"
> "How come I can't drive to Portland?"
> "Why can't I stay out later?"
> "How are you supposed to know what you want to be
>   in life?"

Part of me, I admit, longs for those days when life was
simpler and, even if I didn't have the answer, I could fake it.
Part of me longs for the days when, even if my joke wasn't
funny, the kids would still laugh. Part of me longs for the
days when we would lie there looking at that ceiling sky, and
almost believe the stars were real.

But one of the glories of God's world is change, be it a
hardened heart that warms to His touch, the first spring
blossom of a dogwood tree, or a father who plays many different parts in this multi-act play called parenting.

It is spring, and I am not the father I used to be. And that
is the way it should be.

THE COCAINE KID:
PART III

The news of Norm Edland joining his son in the drug-dealing business and Norm's subsequent suicide was a double whammy, the likes of which I had never experienced.

What had happened? Danny had gotten out of prison. He was showing signs of finally graduating from the school of self-inflicted, ultra-hard knocks. In his last letter to me, in referring to his forthcoming freedom, he had written, "I just know that it will be so much different than ever before."

What had gone wrong?

A letter from Danny in September 1996, a few months after his father's death, answered some of those questions. The return address was a new prison, his fifth.

> I am sure that you are disappointed by the return address, but please do not be. I am feeling more peace than ever. I was full of shame and false pride and that is why you did not hear from me. I am sorry.
>
> I had a neighbor out on the streets who no matter how many times I told him to leave me alone, would not. He and his wife are wonderful God-fearing people who just refused

to let me die, when it was all I wanted. I have so much to tell you. They helped me find what doctors and treatment centers never could. They taught me the Lord loves me and I do not need "things" or "money" to be "somebody." For the first time I really understood your book. I would have written you sooner but when Dad died (and took a lot of me with him), he had your address tucked away.

I praise God each day tenfold for the life I have found (He's given me) but a lot of tragedy is what made it happen. I thought back to when you did that story in 1986, more than ten years ago. How was I to know it had only begun?

Sorry to hear about your father dying. Believe me, I know and feel what you are going through. My father and I got very close while I was in prison. We talked a lot and he was a great support system for me. Prison has a way of taking your self-esteem and my father helped me to keep mine through constant positive conversation. It meant a great deal to me.

It was right when I got out, that the big power jobs of his life were gone. No one wanted to hire him for what he would consider a "good" job. It was right about that time an old "friend" stopped by my work and offered me some drugs at a good price. I did not want them but gave in to the fact that I needed the $500 to $600 I would make by taking it to another "friend."

I truly thought, OK, this one time it was OK. Well, of course, the guy I took them to says, "Can you just do that a few times a week?" I said no at first, but soon thought: Well, it only takes ten minutes out of my day. By the end of the month I had profited around $9,000. Well, Bob, the next month $12,000, after that $18,000, two months after that it was $30,000 a month. And that is when it got so complicated.

My father came to me and said that I was making all this easy money and that he wanted to get involved. I said no way and though he pressed quite a bit, I told him there was always a risk of getting caught and I could just not have him involved. I was giving him money so he did not have

to work that crappy job, and I guess things for him and I
had come full circle:

The kid that always wanted to be like his father now
had a father that wanted to be like his kid.

When I got ready to take a vacation, Dad suggested he
fill in for me while I was gone. I fought it like crazy but decided he could take care of a couple of guys. When I came
home after five days, he had made me about $1,000 a day
and with no trouble.

Between golf in the morning and the pool in the afternoon, he was finding power far greater than he'd ever
known with more money than he could imagine. As a
matter of fact, he had done $60,000 profit so far that month
and it was only the 20th.

While I was gone a guy got busted and set up my Dad.
All the fun and games were over. One night six months later
he called to tell me that nothing in the world could ever
mean what Brienna (granddaughter) and I mean to him.
Twenty minutes later he was dead, a single shot to the head.

It did not seem like he had a friend in the world. He
could not handle it. Twelve hours later we were to be sentenced for our crime. From day one he had no intention of
going through with the sentencing. He had talked to me for
months about us doing it together. He told me I would
never again in life have that kind of money or the freedom
that came with it. But I had a three-year-old daughter who
was going to lose her grandpa and I was not about to have
her suffer anymore.

I admit I was very close to committing suicide and sev-
eral times almost did, but the thought that there was something else for my life kept hounding me. A neighbor (who is
now like family) who knew nothing of what had gone on
kept coming to me, saying, "You need the Lord, my friend"
and it was affecting my heart.

They say all things happen for a reason, and with time I
am trying to piece together what it all means. You said in
your letter that you pray I've learned whatever lesson God
needs me to learn. I know I can say He is the reason I am

alive today to even tell you all this. Praise God, for I give Him all the glory.

Please keep me in your prayers, Bob, for I truly believe the Lord has different plans for me. Take care, my friend. I want to leave you with something that fills me and I use in my time of need:

I Asked God

I asked God for strength, that I might achieve.
I was made weak, that I might learn to obey.
I asked God for health, that I might do greater things.
I was given infirmity, that I might do better things.
I asked for riches, that I might be happy.
I was given poverty, that I might be wise.
I asked for power, that I might have the praise of men.
I was given weakness, that I might feel the need of God.
I asked for all things, that I might enjoy life.
I was given life, that I might enjoy all things.
I got nothing that I asked for.
Almost despite myself, my unspoken prayers were
    answered.
I am, among all men, most richly blessed.

Your friend, Danny

A SILENT
SPRING

As we walk down the hallways, I experience one of those been-here-before sensations. Not here, in this McMinnville, Oregon, nursing home, per se. But in others. The same smell: the aromatic remnants of a chicken dinner and diapers that need changing. The same people, hunched in their wheelchairs. "Help me . . . please help me." The same sense of futility, as if we've come to some sort of human archive where what gives everyone here value is not who they *are* but who they *were*.

But as I follow George Hudson, the setting also reminds me of Dolphus Weary, the man in Mississippi, hurrying me down the hallways of a hospital. Once at our destination, he had pointed me to an infant in his wife's arms. "This," said Mr. Weary, "is my son."

On this rainy March night, Mr. Hudson is not in a hurry. He has come not as a proud father, but as a dutiful son. We enter a room where a man in a bed, eyes closed, is babbling incoherently. On the other side of a curtain, asleep with his mouth open, is the man we've come to see. "This," says Mr. Hudson, "is my father."

George Hudson is 73. His father, William, is 94. But though he's a grandfather who has qualified for the senior-citizen discounts for more than a decade, George is still a son. A son who reminds me how vast is the landscape of this father-son relationship. For this father and son, and for many like them, the Second Spring bears little resemblance to the first. It is a season marked not by a recent beginning—birth—but by an inevitable ending—death. It is a strikingly different season for the two men, a time when a son takes care of the man who once took care of him.

This is a side of fatherhood you don't find on greeting cards. There is nothing warm and fuzzy about a 73-year-old son coming to sit beside his 94-year-old father three times a week in a nursing home. Not when the father cannot talk. Not when the father doesn't even know who his visitor is. But there is something noble about it, particularly when the attendants tell you how most fathers like William Hudson rarely, if ever, get visits from their sons.

This is a silent spring, in which little is said but much is felt. "Doing OK, Dad?" says George, touching the man on the head. He knows his father will not answer; he never answers anymore. But George still feels a need to ask.

On the wall, computer-generated birthday wishes hang next to a photo of an old milk truck, a juxtaposition of generations. George's father once drove such a truck. In fact, George's father once drove a horse-drawn milk wagon in Detroit in the 1920s.

George takes out a photograph. In it, George, perhaps three years old, is sitting atop the horse, Jerry, that did the milk route each day, his father standing to the side. "He told me that horse knew the route so well that it knew which houses to stop at and which not to," said George, chuckling. "I'm not sure what it did when he got a new customer."

The family moved west, to California. George charts the years by jobs, by wars, by moves. He remembers the weekend "over-the-line" baseball games with his father in

Griffith Park in Los Angeles, and the time the two came to blows when George smarted off as a teenager. But the in-between stuff, the bulk of their experience, was the kind of father-son relationship most men of his generation remember: a father whose energy went to bringing in money and rendering discipline.

"My father and I actually became closer once I'd gotten married and had children," remembers George. "He and Mom were wonderful grandparents. We had our tussles. But the older you get, the more you look back and think: Dad was right."

The difficulties for George's parents came in the early eighties when they were having trouble living on their own. George and his wife, Darleen, asked his parents to move from California to Eugene, Oregon, to be near them.

"It was a confusing time for my father," says George. "It was just plain hard."

But the couple moved. As his parents' health deteriorated, more tough decisions had to be made. They had to be moved from a duplex to a nursing home. Then George's father, because he wandered so easily, had to be moved to a separate wing. In 1993, George's mother died. The two had been married 72 years.

"He'd cry," says George. "It was tough."

When George and his wife moved from Eugene to McMinnville, about eighty miles apart, they moved his father to a nursing home near them. Occasionally, they would have him over to the house. "He wouldn't want to leave," says George. "He'd say: 'Don't take me back.' But we had to. We couldn't give him the care he needed."

Compounding the problem was George's own health. In 1994, he had to have triple heart-bypass surgery. Meanwhile, his father had a stroke and now doesn't appear to recognize George or his wife. But still they make their usual three visits a week.

"He's the only thing left of my past," says George. "All of his brothers and sisters are dead. When he goes, it's the end of an era."

Each visit is essentially the same for George: Say hello. Pat his father on the head. Ask a few questions that George knows won't be answered. Sit and look at him—the man who once delivered milk from a horse-drawn cart who now, seven decades later, lies just down from a visitor's area that has magazines with stories on cyberspace and human cloning. Finally, after 15 to 20 minutes, George leaves, almost always feeling guilty about something over which he has no control. What should he do? Not come see his father? Pretend he doesn't exist—the way some sons do with their fathers?

If this is not the stuff Hallmark sells, it is the gritty stuff of fathers and sons. It is a reminder of commitment to the end, bitter though it may be.

Note: William Hudson died April 23, 1997, a month after this visit from his son.

OUT OF THE ASHES

I n Washington's Cascade Mountains, the newspaper photographer and I pulled our car to the side of the dirt road, stepped outside, and scanned what was left of Mount Saint Helens after the May 18, 1980, volcanic eruption: utter bleakness.

We had come to this spot in southwestern Washington to report on the aftermath of an explosion whose force was more powerful than any atomic bomb ever tested. The once-graceful peak lay in jagged heaps, 1300 feet of the mountain having been blown off. Downed trees in the distance looked like scattered matchsticks. Spirit Lake, once a deep blue jewel on which canoes glided past woodsy cabins, was now a primordial greenish-gray. No birds sang. No wildlife scurried. The scene was eerily still, suggesting death.

And for good reason: 57 people had been killed in the explosion. Some victims were enveloped in hot gases that traveled at hurricane speeds—450 miles per hour, leaving no sign of wildlife for 150 square miles in the weeks afterward.

Ash had spewed 60,000 feet in the air, some of it circling the globe for years. Rivers were turned to funnels of mud.

222 • A FATHER FOR ALL SEASONS

Logging trucks lay twisted like a toddler's toys mangled by the family car.

It looked like a war zone.

But as I surveyed this landscape of destruction, something small and seemingly insignificant caught my attention: a twig of columbine poking through the ash. And not far away, a few patches of sword ferns rising in the rubble.

They were reminders of healing. Reminders of hope. Indeed, within three years of the blast, 90 percent of the plants common to the area had reestablished themselves. Elk and deer populations had returned to normal levels in all but the hardest-hit areas. And most of the 53 lakes and 298 miles of streams affected by the eruption were resurrecting themselves.

There is a time to heal, says Ecclesiastes. And in Second Spring, that healing goes well beyond nature, to people. To fathers and sons, sometimes after explosions have turned their relational landscape into something that looks like a war zone.

● ● ●

It happened in what may have seemed like an ordinary, happy suburban family in Dayton, Ohio in the sixties. But looking back, Jeff Schulte, now 35, remembers a childhood like this:

> I can still picture my dad bouncing me on his knee, coaching me in Little League, showing me how to shine my shoes, helping me reel in my first fish, and telling me stories about his early days as an undercover detective on the Dayton Police force.
>
> I can still hear him saying the words, "Son, I love you." I can imagine him messing up my hair, wrestling me on the living room floor, and sharing a hot dog with me at a Cincinnati Reds game.
>
> I can still see him puffing up his chest when he talked about me to his friends. He was proud to be my

dad. He would do anything for me—I was *his* son and he was *my* dad. I was a chip off the old block.

Thus was the childhood Jeff longed to remember. But it was a childhood that lived only in the imagination of someone so starved for father-love that he decided fake memories were better than facing the real thing.

What really happened: When Jeff was three, his father left his mother for a woman he met in a bar a mile from their house. The man walked out on his wife and six children, ranging from age 14 to three months.

When that relationship faltered, he remarried Jeff's mom. "I remember my mom asking us if we wanted him to come home again," remembers Jeff. "Of course we did."

But after returning, the man left again in nine months for the same woman, this time for good. Jeff's mother raised the family on her own.

Jeff saw his father again only twice in the next two decades—when he was 11 and 25. The man showed up for a daughter's graduation and another daughter's wedding, then was gone.

Meanwhile, Jeff won an academic scholarship and played football at Yale, from which he graduated in 1984. He got married. He joined Campus Crusade for Christ. But college and marriage and ministry and literally decades with no significant contact with his father couldn't dilute Jeff's sense that he needed to somehow reconnect.

In 1989, at age 29, he decided he must see his father. He drove from Little Rock, Arkansas, to Sheboygan, Wisconsin, arriving in a snowstorm. And, at his father's workplace, he sat alone with the man who had left him and the rest of the family. He did not confront him. He did not chastise him. Instead, he had the strangest desire to reach out and touch the man's hands.

He looked his father in the eye and asked: "Do you love me?"

"Of course I love you," said his father.

"Did you miss me?"

"Of course I missed you," said his father.

"I needed to hear that," said Jeff.

Then he touched his father's hands. "As soon as I touched his hands, I knew why I wanted to do that. Because those were the hands that I had dreamed and imagined would hold me and tickle me and toss me around a room. Those were the hands that I always imagined wrapping around mine, to show me how to swing a bat, how to catch a ball."

But until that moment, in 1989, those hands were never there for Jeff. For some sons, that reality, festering over time, leads to bitterness. For Jeff, however, it led only to longing. And a desire to heal the wound. Before he left Wisconsin, he told his father: "I'm a chip off the old block."

His father, he came to learn, had been raised by a philanderer of a father and an alcoholic mother; he had left home at 17. "My dad," said Jeff, "simply gave me what his dad gave him. It was as if he were living life in a wheelchair. I couldn't suddenly demand that he get up and walk."

Instead, Jeff decided all he could do was love his father with the love of Christ. As he did so, the brittleness between father and son began softening. And that softening spread to his siblings, some of whom vowed they could never forgive the man who had hurt them so badly. But they did.

In the summer of 1996, when his father's wife died, Jeff's brothers and sisters were reunited with their dad. For the first time, Jeff's father broke down and wept. He admitted he had betrayed his wife and children. On the invitation of his children, he moved back to Dayton to be closer to them.

"It was the first time I had ever seen my mother and my father together in the same living room," said Jeff. "He had 17 grandchildren he needed to get to know. We gave him 17 5 x 7 pictures to help him with the names."

A while later, Jeff, his father, and two brothers played

nine holes of golf together. On the last green, Jeff gathered the group and told them to stop and drink in this moment. Did they realize, he asked, how amazing this was?

"I can't believe how all six of you kids have forgiven me," said his father. "It's unreal."

"It is unreal," said Jeff. "All of us are experiencing unreal love and unreal forgiveness from a very real God. What's going on is bigger than your kids, Dad. It's about a God in heaven who gives second chances, who wants you to experience His love and His forgiveness."

Looking back, Jeff considers his mother "one of God's heroes," a woman who refused to give up even when left to raise six children on her own. And he finds himself occasionally angry when he considers the 30 years without his father. "What a waste," he says. "What a waste."

But in the end, he had to get beyond his anger to the hurt. Had to realize that in setting someone else free, we find we were actually the prisoner. "I thought a mountain range separated me and my dad, but it was actually just a curb. I'm not saying there weren't issues, but forgiveness is all that separated us."

Now a speaker for Family Life Conferences and living in Nashville with his wife and four young children, Jeff recently spoke at a church in Dayton. In walked his father. Though his father was nearly 70 years old, until that day he had never attended an event his son had been involved in, be it a graduation, a game, a speech.

"I wasn't there for you then," his father told him recently. "I am now."

Sometimes father-son relationships explode with atomic-energy force, leaving once-graceful peaks scattered in jagged heaps, leaving a scene of devasation, leaving little sign of hope for the rejuvenation of life.

"But it is never too late," said a little boy whose father was lost but now is found. "Never."

STILL A SON

S ails down, I nudged our 22-foot boat quietly into the moorage. A wisp of campground smoke hovered above the lake. Children laughed as they played along the shoreline. And, for a moment, I was 12 years old again, proudly landing the boat after an August evening of fly-fishing with my father.

But in reality I was 43 years old, and my father wasn't there. It was just me and my mother, ending a sail we had taken to commemorate the first anniversary of his death.

The evening had not been particularly emotional for me, even though I had sailed with the man for nearly three decades, from the time the two of us built a ten-foot pram with a bed-sheet sail. And, briefly, I felt guilty about that. Shouldn't this day have hit me harder than it did? Could I really have cared about him as much as I thought I did? Was it sacrilegious to spend the evening sailing—even laughing on occasion—rather than mourning for the man?

It has been that kind of year: A year of questions. A year of contemplation. A year of walking a twisting trail in the dark, thinking you see a guiding blaze in this tree or that tree but not really sure. Because when you lose your father, nobody hands you a map that shows where you're going and how you're supposed to get there.

Racked with guilt, some sons never even find the trailhead when their fathers die. *I should have . . . I could have . . . I never told him . . .*

Burning with bitterness, some sons try to forget him and blaze their own trail. *He never did this with me . . . He never said that to me . . . He only thought of himself . . .*

Mired in indifference, some sons wander aimlessly in the mid-life wilderness. *He wasn't the best of fathers . . . He wasn't the worst of fathers . . . But he's gone now, so what difference does it make?*

Me? I've followed a trail that took a number of unexpected turns: the anniversaries and places and events that I thought would hurt so much, have not. My first trip to the sailboat after he died . . . his birthday . . . taking home tools that belonged to him—I took such events in stride.

But sometimes when I was walking confidently down the path—boom—I'd suddenly trip and fall flat. A few weeks after he died, I was trying to finish a kitchen add-on project that I'd begun six months before. It was late at night. It was hot. I was tired. And when a nearby bed sheet caught in an electric grinder—don't even ask—I fell to pieces. I ripped off my tool belt and ran into the night, tears mixing with the sawdust that covered my face.

I wasn't thinking about how tired I was or how frustrated I was or how I was going to explain to my friend Jason that I'd jammed his grinder with a bed sheet. No, I was thinking how lonely I felt because my father was gone. I was feeling strangely like a little boy who had had something good taken from him and felt cheated.

A few weeks later, I experienced another meltdown after running across an old letter my father had written and seeing the bold X's and O's he would scrawl beneath his signature. I called the newspaper where I work and said I wouldn't be in. And, of course, felt guilty for doing so.

Real men don't grieve. Real men don't hurt. Real men don't ask for help. But I felt as if I were having an emotional heart attack. I needed a spiritual EMT.

"Could you call Rick," I asked my wife, "and see if he can come over?"

Rick Taylor is more than the pastor of the church we attend. He's one of my closest friends. And having experienced the drowning of his 5-year-old son, Kyle, he not only understands death, but has written about it with amazing insight in his book *When Life Is Changed Forever.* He arrived within an hour.

When I could muster the strength to move my mouth, I asked him why I was still hurting like this. "My father lived a long and mostly happy life. My pain isn't like my brother-in-law's. He lost a 16-year-old son; I had 42 years with my dad. I had closure. The last thing I did was hug him and tell him I loved him. So why can't I get over this?"

Rick answered the question with one of his own. "How long does it take a man with one arm to get over the loss of his arm?" he asked.

"But," I countered, "though we got along well, my father and I were very different people. Though I loved him, he wasn't the hero that some sons see their father as. And it wasn't like he was around every day, like a spouse or child or even a close friend."

"He was your *dad*," said Rick. "Even though the two of you were different, who you are is linked directly to who he was. He will always be a part of you. You're flesh of his flesh. And so when he's suddenly not around, you're going to feel something's missing. Why? Because something *is* missing. And it's okay to miss that something—that someone."

On Father's Day—my first without a dad—I was minutes away from giving the guest sermon at our church when I looked at the flower arrangement my wife had placed in front of the lectern. With her ability to add just the right personal touch, she had placed the flowers in an old fishing creel of my father's. And though I had been unemotional to that point, I looked at that creel and crumbled.

But as I buried my face in my hands, I felt a reassuring hand patting my shoulder. It belonged to my 15-year-old son, Jason, who seemed to be saying: *It's okay, Dad. We understand.* In that moment, that's exactly what I needed: Someone to say it was okay. Someone to say it was okay to hurt even if the man had been dead for ten months.

Other than God's healing touch, having the permission to hurt—from my wife, children, pastor, friends, and church —was what got me through this year. Because when you lose a father, I found, he sometimes becomes more real to you than when he was while alive.

In the past 12 months, I've probably thought of him— pondered him—more than at any other time of my life, and not just because I was writing this book. I thought of him when I coached my last season of kids' baseball and he wasn't there, sitting in his lawn chair, to root on his grandson. When Mom and I pulled the sailboat out of the lake last fall and I had to take apart all his inventive fittings, some of which I still haven't quite figured out. And when I was flying over the Cascade Mountains last May and suddenly realized one of the bodies of water below was Cultus Lake, where our family vacationed every summer when I was a kid.

As I marveled at the surreal scene below—the lakes we fished, the trails we hiked, the woods we carved miniature golf courses in—I saw it: Well off the beaten trail, a lake shaped like a comma. The mysterious lake Dad and I had seen on the map and searched for from time to time but never been able to find: Comma Lake.

And I wanted to say: *Dad, there it is. I've found it. Comma Lake does exist! We weren't nuts after all!* When I looked next to me, though, I saw only a businessman, fast asleep.

Which hurt. But, I'm learning, that's all right. Feeling loss suggests something good: that my father and I had something worth losing. We explored life together. We shared experiences together. We communicated together. And so losing him must, necessarily, be painful. Don't pity the man who loses a father and hurts; pity the man who loses a father and doesn't. Pain is the privilege of having something worth losing.

So I've tried not to run from the man, to pretend he didn't exist, as some sons try to do. I refuse to stow his memory in some dark attic, where it can't be reached. I refuse to add up his faults, hoping that the equation will equal less pain. At work, I've pinned to my bulletin board that final photo taken of us only moments before I said goodbye to him for the last time. Not long ago, I even talked Mom into taking me back to the old gym at Corvallis High to show me where they had met in September 1942.

I've tried to appreciate the good things he passed on to me and to overcome his shortcomings; his fiberglass-encased paintbrush is displayed prominently in my office, not to ridicule the man's lack of follow-through but to remind myself to complete life's tasks.

One of those tasks is accepting the reality that you're never finished being a son; death removes a person, not a relationship. For better or worse, fathers and sons are still connected by strands of shared experiences, memories, and genes.

Death does change the role of an adult son, however. Instantaneously I felt older, less innocent; as a boyhood friend told me when he heard about my father's death—the first such loss among my "old gang":

"I guess this means we're not kids anymore."

I suddenly found myself with a heightened responsibility for my mother, who turned 70 last spring; together, we have learned and grown closer, mainly in trying to dismantle, reassemble, and sail a boat with about 22,000 movable parts, but also in dealing with one another's emotions, which may be no less complex.

I also sense an urgency to make the most of the time I have with my own sons. As a little boy, I thought my father was invincible. As an adult, I realized he was not; and yet even when my sister called that morning and told me the

EMTs were working on my father, my first thought was that I might miss a couple days work as he recuperated in the hospital. I never thought he would die. But he did. As we all will.

During this last year, though, I have learned something about death. It can destroy the body, but it cannot touch the things that matter most. Not memories. Not legacies. Not continuation for those left behind. For in the language of life, the death of a father is poignant punctuation that signals a pause, separating two subjects and forever changing the cadence of the words that follow—but also suggesting that the sentence is not over.

Death is not a period. It's a comma. The man is still my father. And I am still his son.

LETTING GO

4:30-4:45 P.M.
Goodbyes

It's time for a last get-together with your parents. Now is a good time to say goodbye—at least for a while.

—From the 1997-98 Orientation Day booklet
Linfield College
McMinnville, Oregon

E ver since the booklet arrived in July, the paragraph had irritated me like a speck of dirt under my contact lens: a small matter that clouded everything I saw, including a summer whose ending I dreaded. August 30, the day Ryan was to leave for school, became a benchmark draped in black, a specter of change that I didn't want to confront.

Now that day had arrived. Ryan and my wife headed north in his car for the two-hour trip; I followed in another.

Having children, I've decided, is like buying something on the no-payment-till-August plan. When you say yes, you never stop to think that a bill will actually arrive someday.

You think only of how much you will enjoy the item right now. But in my life as a father, my payment was due. Eighteen years after walking out into that starry Central Oregon night thinking *I'm a father*, a bill arrived that said *Now is a good time to say goodbye. . . .* The price you pay for being a parent, I've learned, is having to let go.

True, Ryan was moving only 85 miles away, not across the country; I knew fathers whose sons were going across the country or into the military. Still, those 85 miles would change our relationship like nothing else. This transition would be more than a separation of distance; it would also be a changing of roles. I would become less necessary to my son's life.

As our two-car caravan continued toward Linfield College and 4:45 P.M., I kept thinking about that "good time to say goodbye" phrase. Is there really such thing as a good time to say goodbye to a kid you once rocked, cuddled, and pulled on your golf cart as if he were a jockey riding a horse? A kid with whom you've camped, fished, sailed, skied, sledded, run, read, laughed, wept, and prayed? With whom you've played football, basketball, baseball, tennis, golf, ping pong, hide-and-seek, and way too many games of Candy Land? Who, a few weeks before, had left a note of encouragement in your shoe for a relay race you were running?

Like his father, he hadn't been perfect. But time had tempered any transgressions, including the time years ago when he used my beloved copper wedge as a hockey stick. Now, everthing was changing.

I had hoped to spend more time with him in this final summer before college, but he worked evenings and I worked days. When he wasn't working, he was practicing golf. He was determined to win the men's club championship at the public golf course where he played and worked, an exceedingly lofty goal for a young man who had just made the transition from junior tournaments to men's tournaments and had never won a championship of any kind.

"Dad," he had told me, "I'm going to win it."

Where had this summer gone? I asked myself as I headed toward Linfield. *Where had 18 years of fatherhood gone?* It seemed as if I were watching a fast-forwarded movie, as if just yesterday I had taken photos of 5-year-old Ryan and 2-year-old Jason leaning against the goalposts at halftime of a Linfield football game.

Now, I found myself feeling like a contractor who has just poured a huge foundation and is worried that the fast-drying cement will permanently fix all the mistakes he's made. Or like the harried mom who is packing her kid for camp, worrying that something will get left out of the suitcase.

I contemplated writing Ryan one final fatherly-advice opus in which I could impart to him all that I believe he needs to remember. But then I caught myself. I've been writing that opus, I realize, for the last 18 years. And despite spelling errors and grammatical goofs, it will have to suffice.

To cram his head now with a list of "do's" and "don'ts" would speak more of a desperate father trying to run a hurry-up offense than of a trusting father who realizes that an 18-year-old must develop his own faith, hope, and dreams—a game plan of his own.

And that, in a sense, is what the theme of this father-son opus should be: trust. Not just between us, but *beyond* us. Who my son becomes in the next four or five years, I believe, will hinge on one question: In whom, or what, will he place his ultimate trust?

Will he trust in money or materialism or the media or the majority or famous people or politicians or liberalism or conservatism or management or unions or trends or science or jobs or political correctness or the status quo? I hope he doesn't trust completely in any of those things. I don't even want him trusting totally in the education he's about to receive or in religion or in me or in himself.

What I hope he trusts in above all else is this: the matchless grace of God. In the One to whom he really belongs. In the One who has promised to never abandon us, the ultimate Father for all seasons.

As freeways and city turned to farms and country roads, I remembered how, just a week before, our family had gathered for a short vacation amid the stately pines of Central Oregon. While playing golf one day, I noticed Ry had written "Psalm 20:7" on his bag-tag, which suggested he's not building his house on sand. "Some trust in chariots and some in horses," reads the verse, "but we trust in the name of the Lord our God."

That evening, the two of us prowled the rough for golf balls on this high-mountain course, not far from where my father had died the year before. It was a rare time of us being alone together, walking amid the towering ponderosas and the knee-high saplings that would someday replace them.

There was so much I wanted to tell him, but some things are hard to say. In the evening quiet—and with no particular eloquence—I simply told him how proud his mother and I were of him, how eager we were to see him soar on his own, and how the most important thing he could do while at college was to heed that bag-tag advice.

On the eve of his departure, I left him a going-away present in his bedroom. I had considered lots of gifts, but only one seemed like the right choice: the copper wedge.

When Ry was small, I had used the club to show him how to play this game. Later, we shared the hockey-nicked club during rounds played together. But lately, it had spent more time in his bag than mine, which only seemed right; he had made better use of it than I had. And that, I think, is the hope of most of us fathers: that our sons will take what's been handed down to them and make more of it than we did.

Alone on the country roads, I found myself thinking back to a gift my father had given me when I had left for college: A used Nikkormat camera. A commercial photographer, he had always been the picture-taker in our family. So the gift, I realize now, was more than an organized collection of metal, shutter, screws, and lenses. It was encouragement to see the world through my own eyes. It was permission. It was freedom to focus on whatever I wanted.

As the mileposts flashed past, the image settled deep within me, stirring some new thought. By the time I linked with Sally and Ry on the Linfield campus, I had realized something I had missed in my poor-me mood of summer:

If letting go is the price parents pay for raising children, it is also the dividend. Not because of some cynical notion that children somehow confine us and, thus, separation untangles us, but because letting go is not the end of the parent-child story. It is the fulfilled purpose of parenting: to send into the world children who can live without us.

A writer once said that although an author may labor for months, sometimes years, a book is never really finished. At some point it must be handed over to a publisher to be printed, but it is never really ready. That's the way it is with children, I think. They're never really ready. But at some point, they must be handed over to other people, other places, and other experiences—to complete the process God allowed us to begin.

"There are two lasting bequests we can give our children," wrote Hodding Carter Jr., the Pulitzer-Prize winning Mississippi editor, "One is roots. The other is wings."

When I taught Ryan to play golf I gave him roots; when I stepped aside and let him embrace the game on his own terms, not mine, I gave him wings. And watched as he soared from a kid struggling to make the school JV team to, at 18, the youngest men's club champion in our public course's history. At summer's end, he won that men's club tournament he so desperately wanted to win, chipping in for an eagle during a sudden-death playoff.

Now, on a broader scale, it was time again to step aside and let my son fly, just as Whistlin' Willie had once done for his son, just as my father had once done for me, just as fathers everywhere would be doing for their sons in the September weeks to come. It was time to experience a new season, in which I still would be a father, but a father with a different role.

The clock struck 4:45 P.M. and my world did not end. In a dorm room decorated in Neo-Tiger (as in Woods), I hugged my son goodbye. No cymbals. No profound words of wisdom. Misty eyes, but no tears. Instead, just a few awkward moments in which the silence said more than the stilted words—and the hurt seemed somehow necessary, as if a rite of passage into this Second Spring.

As fathers and sons, our lives are filled with such symbols of transition: A cry from the maternity ward. A first baseball game together. A handshake instead of a goodnight kiss. A soccer ball that will never again be kicked. A hug that seals reconciliation. A 5 A.M. phone call.

With a rhythm all their own, father-son seasons come and go, blessing us, grieving us, teaching us, and leaving us all the richer for having been part of this purpose under heaven.